DECCAN HERITAGE
FOUNDATION

Striving to promote and implement the preservation and conservation of the historic monuments and cultural heritage of the Deccan within a holistic environment and social context

Deccan Heritage Foundation Ltd
Suite, 1, 3rd Floor, 11-12 St James's
Square, London SW1Y 4LB, UK

12A Delstar, 9/9A Hughes Road,
Kemps Corner, Mumbai 400 036

www.deccanheritagefoundation.org

© **TEXT** George Michell and Gethin Rees
© **PHOTOGRAPHY** Surendra Kumar

DESIGN Nidhi Sah
PRINTING JAK Printers Pvt Ltd

ISBN 978-93-86867-04-9
First Jaico Impression 2017

PUBLISHED BY
Jaico Publishing House
A-2 Jash Chambers,
7-A Sir Phirozshah Mehta Road
Fort, Mumbai - 400 001
jaicopub@jaicobooks.com
www.jaicobooks.com

PREVIOUS PAGE
Nashik, Pandu
Lena, *Chaitya*
(Cave 18), facade

OPPOSITE
Karla, *Chaitya*
(Cave 8),
wall panel of
mithuna couple

FOLLOWING
PAGES

PAGE 4
Bedsa, *Chaitya*
(Cave 7),
columns with
bell-shaped
capitals and
brackets carved
with horse riders

PAGE 5
Karla, *Chaitya*
(Cave 8), column
bracket with
elephant riders

BUDDHIST ROCK-CUT MONASTERIES
OF THE WESTERN GHATS

George Michell
24 X 2017

The Deccan Heritage Foundation would like to acknowledge the generous support of
John and **Fausta Eskenazi** in bringing out this publication.

BUDDHIST ROCK-CUT MONASTERIES
OF THE WESTERN GHATS

GEORGE MICHELL AND GETHIN REES

PHOTOGRAPHY Surendra Kumar

JAICO PUBLISHING HOUSE
Ahmedabad Bangalore Bhopal Bhubaneswar Chennai
Delhi Hyderabad Kolkata Lucknow Mumbai

DECCAN HERITAGE
FOUNDATION

CONTENTS

FOREWORD

The story of the Buddhist rock-cut monasteries of the Western Ghats begins in the kingdom of ancient Magadha during the reigns of the Maurya emperor Ashoka and his grandson Dashratha in the 3rd century BCE. At this time seven rock-cut caves were excavated in the Barabar and Nagarjuni hills near Gaya in ancient Bihar. The trend gained momentum and spread to Orissa, down to Andhra Pradesh and Karnataka, and then towards western Maharashtra where rock-cut architecture reached its zenith. While much has been written about Ajanta and Ellora, here, George Michell, an eminent architecture historian, and the young archaeologist Gethin Rees have together traced the history of the lesser known, but important Buddhist monasteries in this part of India in a very focused and interesting manner. Their passion and hard work has brought unexplored facets of these monasteries to the fore providing renewed perspective. For example, they explain in detail how the geography of the Deccan Trap exerted a critical influence on the economy and culture of the region, and how the diverse coastline of the Konkan offered numerous safe ports, thereby facilitating trade, commerce and trans-ocean contacts across the Arabian Sea.

    The authors take the reader on a lucid journey through the history of the various dynasties that contributed to the excavation of these magnificent monuments, from the Satavahanas and Kshatrapas, to the Vakatakas and Rashtrakutas, rulers who all participated in the continuation and prosperity of these Buddhist centres over a period of more than 1,000 years. It is interesting to note how the funding of

PREVIOUS PAGES
Karla, *Chaitya* (Cave 8), from James Fergusson and James Burgess, *The Cave Temples of India*

BELOW
Kondane, *Chaitya* (Cave 1), wall panels with dancing figures

rock-cutting actually took place, how revenue was generated for clothes and food for monks and nuns, and to what extent the management of finances and administration was worked out to the smallest detail. The interaction between the Buddhist community, traders and rural folk through feasts and ceremonies is very well described.

In this guidebook the authors analyse the mystery of the origins of rock-cut architecture. They offer explanations for how the excavations were carried out to achieve perfectly designed spaces with column alignments of extraordinary precision, all with the help of rudimentary iron tools such as hammers, axes and chisels. The section on sculpture describes various recurrent motifs like the *bodhi* tree and the *dharmachakra*, and the images of Buddha and the Bodhisattvas, as well as the significance and occurrence of each of these in the different monastic shrines and residences.

This guidebook will be useful not only for research scholars but for all visitors interested in rock-cut architecture, especially those monuments in western Maharashtra. I have known George Michell from my school days, when he was a close friend of my father Dr. Suresh Vasant, and first met Gethin Rees in 2005, and ever since we have exchanged views on rock-cut architecture. It is therefore a great honour and a pleasure to write this Foreword.

Dr. Shreekant Jadhav,
Former Deputy Director,
Directorate of Archaeology & Museums, Government of Maharashtra

AUTHORS' PREFACE

The rugged ranges of the Western Ghats in Maharashtra are home to some of the most ancient monuments in India. Known popularly as "caves", these are not natural grottos, but, rather, man-made excavations laboriously hewn from top to bottom into sheer cliff faces. They were fasioned between the 2nd-1st centuries BCE and the 5th-6th centuries CE as places of worship and residence for the Buddhist monastic communities active in this part of India, at this early time in the religion's history. While Buddhism was exported to neighbouring countries, where it continues to flourish to this day, the religion gradually disappeared from its country of origin. As a result, Buddhist establishments across India, including the rock-cut monasteries described in this guidebook, came to be neglected, abandoned and then altogether forgotten until rediscovered in the 18th and 19th centuries by artists and antiquarians. Since then, scholars have translated inscriptions on the monuments and documented their architectural features and sculptures. Though this has led to a better understanding of the early dynastic and religious history of the Deccan the dating of many caves remains uncertain (see pages 124-5).

While the Buddhist caves at Ajanta and Ellora in the vicinity of Aurangabad in northern Maharashtra are the best-known rock-cut monuments of this type in the Deccan, they are not included here. Instead, this volume concentrates on the less familiar, but no less significant Buddhist monasteries of the Western Ghats and the adjacent Konkan coastal region bordering the Arabian Sea. Easily accessible to visitors from Mumbai, Pune or Nashik, the caves are today under the protection of Central and State Government Archaeological Departments and are open to the public seven days a week. That said, several of the caves described here are somewhat remotely located, and visiting them requires strenuous climbs and even treks through forested wilderness populated by leopards! It is hoped that this guidebook, illustrated with the splendid photographs of Surendra Kumar, will encourage visitors to seek out these testaments to the skill of the masons and sculptors of ancient India, and to the dedication of the patrons who inspired their wondrous creation.

Junnar,
Manmodi Hill,
Bhimshankar
Group, view
from the *Chaitya*
(Cave 2)

THE SETTING

THE WESTERN GHATS

RULING DYNASTIES

TRADE AND COMMERCE

BUDDIST COMMUNITIES AND THEIR PATRONS

The Western Ghats

THE WESTERN GHATS

Three distinct terrains characterise the geography of what is now western Maharashtra, the region in which all the Buddhist rock-cut monasteries described in this guidebook are located. From east to west these are: the elevated Deccan plateau; the Western Ghats; and the Konkan coastal strip wedged between the foothills of the Ghats and the Arabian Sea coast. These distinct landscapes are home to more than 50 individual groups of monasteries, including those in the vicinity of Nashik and Junnar, surrounded by outlying ranges of the Western Ghats; those of Karla, Bhaja, Bedsa and Kondane, on the edges of steep-sided river valleys in the very heart of the Western Ghats; and in the Konkan, those of Kanheri and Mahakala (Kondivte), now subsumed within greater metropolitan Mumbai, as well as Kuda. The area covered by these sites extends almost 200 kilometres from north to south, and about 120 kilometres from east to west.

The Western Ghats in this part of Maharashtra are punctuated by dramatic craggy peaks, many rising more than 1,000 metres above sea level, the tallest being Kalsubai, soaring to 1,650 metres. Formed during the Tertiary Era around 50 to 80 million years ago, this topography is composed of horizontally laid sheets of basalt created by numerous lava flows. Time and weathering have eroded this stone mass into mountains with tiers of sheer cliffs. Hence the Swedish term *trap* (as in "Deccan Trap"), as well as the Indian term *ghat*, both meaning "steps", referring to the stepped rock formations characteristic of these ranges. Because of the restrictions this terrain imposed on the movement of peoples and goods travelling up from the Konkan coast through rugged mountain passes like Nana Ghat to the Deccan plateau, the geography of the Western Ghats has always exerted a critical influence on economy and culture. In turn, this affected the evolution of Buddhist rock-cut architecture, which by its very nature was dependent on local geology. The comparative softness of the basalt, combined with the great thickness and consistency of its superimposed layers, often exposed as vertical faces, proved an ideal environment for the development of rock-cut architecture.

The Konkan littoral is dotted with rocky terraces and cliffs, sand dunes, sand-lined pocket beaches, tidal inlets, creeks and estuaries. This diverse coastline has offered safe anchorages since ancient times, thereby facilitating the trans-ocean contacts across the Arabian Sea that had such a profound impact on the economy of this part of India. The evolution of transport technology during these early centuries led to the development of long-distance travel. Sturdy stitched-timber boats, quite different to those used for coastal sailing, proved suitable for trans-oceanic voyages, especially once the understanding and exploitation of the seasonal monsoon winds had been mastered. This led to the traversal of the Indian Ocean and migration of different peoples and goods, a change that profoundly influenced the development of the architecture and art of the Western Ghats.

RULING DYNASTIES

Footpath cut through Nana Ghat

During the second half of the first millennium BCE, large swathes of northern India were unified at different times into single polities, some of which, like that of the Mauryas, assumed imperial dimensions. At the same time, the Deccan region witnessed processes of urbanisation and state formation that led to the establishment and growth of the Satavahana empire, one of its capitals being the city of Paithan, ancient Pratishthana, on a section of the Godavari river east of the Ghats in central Maharashtra. Epigraphic and numismatic evidence reveals that the Western Ghats and the Konkan lay at the core of the Satavahana world, and that rulers of this dynasty exerted considerable influence on the Deccan when many of the rock-cut monasteries considered here were cut. Thus the history of Satavahanas is relevant to defining the chronology of the monasteries, and to understanding the role of royal figures in supporting Buddhism and its expression in rock-cut architecture and sculpture.

Nashik, Pandu Lena, Cave 10; wall inscription mentioning the Kshatrapa king Nahapana

More than twenty inscriptions found in the monasteries of the Western Ghats mention the Satavahanas, confirming their contemporaneity with certain rulers of this line. But the Satavahana kingdom was not a monolithic state throughout its history. Instead, it was composed of localised polities brought under varying degrees of control at different times by a centralised authority. Piecing together the chronologies of the Satavahanas and lesser kings and queens is problematic since the available historical sources do not agree on names or dates. What seems certain, however, is that the Satavahanas dominated the Deccan for about 400 years, from around the 2nd century BCE to the 3rd century CE. There is considerable scholarly debate regarding Satavahana history, and although the longer chronology has been adopted here for simplicity, events occurring before the 1st century BCE may have actually taken place up to one century later.

The origins of the Satavahanas are unclear, though their ancestors may have been vassals of the Mauryas whose empire extended into peninsular India. Their earliest inscriptions, dating from the 2nd to 1st centuries BCE, are found around Nashik at the edge of the Western Ghats. At some date in the 1st century CE the Kshatrapa king Nahapana invaded the Satavahana territories, leaving a record in Cave 10 at Pandu Lena outside Nashik. The Kshatrapas based their notion of kingship on the Indo-Greek states located in what is now northern Pakistan and Afghanistan. This foreign link is borne out by Kshatrapa coins that often display Greek or pseudo-Greek legends and stylised busts of rulers. The occasional inscriptions found in the monasteries signed by *yavanas*, a general term for foreigners associated with the aforementioned Greek kingdoms, confirm the cosmopolitan character of the region during these centuries.

The Kshatrapas occupied the Deccan for barely half a century, and were eventually expelled from the region by Gautamiputra Satakarni, the greatest of the Satavahanas. By the end of Gautamiputra's reign, around 130 CE, the Satavahana domains extended into Rajasthan in northwestern India, and from Saurashtra in the extreme west to Orissa on the Bay of Bengal to the east. Little wonder that Gautamiputra styled himself as Rajaraja, King of Kings. During the last years of his reign and for some time after his death, his mother, queen Gautami Balashri played a role in the kingdom's administration, and her name is mentioned in Cave 3 at Pandu Lena. The next Satavahana rulers of consequence were Vasishthiputra Pulumavi and Vasishthiputra Satakarni, whose successive reigns spanned much of the 2nd century. In about 140 CE the latter married the daughter of the Kshatrapa king Rudradaman I, an alliance that did not prevent the Kshatrapas from occupying the Deccan once again. However Yajnashri Satakarni, who reigned towards the end of the 2nd century, expelled the

Nashik, Pandu Lena, Cave 3, sponsored by the Satavahana queen Gautami Balashri

Kanheri, *Chaitya* (Cave 3); pillar inscription mentioning the Satavahana king Yajnashri Satakarni

invaders, thereby temporarily reviving the Satavahana fortunes. Yajnashri is credited with personally completing one of the monuments at Pandu Lena (Cave 20); he was on the throne when the forecourt of the great *chaitya* hall (Cave 3) at Kanheri was dedicated.

The western Deccan experienced a period of instability following the waning of Satavahana power in the 3rd century, and it was not until the emergence of the Traikutakas towards the end of the 4th century that a single polity in the region was re-established. That the Traikutakas were contemporaries of the Vakatakas of the central Deccan and the Guptas of northern India helps explain the artistic influences from these zones that flowed to the Western Ghats during the 5th-6th centuries. The next dynasty to dominate the Western Ghats, for about 200 years from the middle of the 8th century, is that of the Rashtrakutas, based in central Maharashtra. However, Rashtrakuta control of the area was probably no more than temporary and tentative. While the name of Amoghavarsha, a mid-9th century Rashtrakuta ruler, is found at Kanheri (Cave 11), this is only mentioned in a record of a prince of the subservient Shilahara family. Other than the monastery at Kanheri, which continued to be inhabited to some extent up until the 12th century, all the other rock-cut sites described in this volume were by this time abandoned.

What need did patronising Buddhist monuments fulfil for royal patrons? Apart from personal beliefs in the virtues of Buddhism and the benefits of acquiring merit by giving, there can be no doubt that sponsorship provided rulers with opportunities to display their power and wealth, as well as satisfying both economic and political needs. Given their locations near long-distance trade routes, Buddhist monasteries in more remote locations were involved with maintaining communications, thereby contributing to the financial welfare of the state. The display of royal support in the form of funding excavations and authoring inscriptions also helped to bolster royal claims to disputed territories. Thus conspicuous patronage of the monasteries at Pandu Lena reflected the Satavahanas' struggle to hold onto nearby Nashik. Once he had regained control of this city for the Satavahanas, Gautamiputra Satakarni and his relatives left records of the former's triumph in Cave 3 at Pandu Lena. Later Satavahana monarchs continued to make donations to the same monastery, evidenced by their names in inscriptions, the grand scale of the excavations and the outstanding quality of the carving.

TRADE AND COMMERCE

The growth of urban settlements in the Deccan during the course of the 1st millennium BCE also impacted on the Buddhist rock-monasteries. Several large settlement mounds at Nashik, Junnar, Karad and Brahmapuri have been discovered on the eastern fringe of the Western Ghats, while Arabian Sea ports like Sopara, Elephanta and Chaul have been identified from archaeological explorations as well as from the *Periplus of the Erythraean Sea*, the Greek navigational manual dating from the 1st century CE. Excavations at these sites provide glimpses into life in the cities of the Satavahana era. Buddhist monuments and urban houses employed burnt bricks of standard size; roofs were of terracotta tiles. Brick-lined ring-wells occur at a number of larger sites, together with an abundance of coins, ceramics, terracotta figurines, glass bangles, beads and metal objects. These diverse objects attest to a range of industries producing a sophisticated and fairly standardised material culture across the western Deccan. Items imported from northern India and even from the further shores of the Indian Ocean attest to the existence of long-distance connections. The bronzes unearthed at Brahmapuri, for instance, include Hellenistic figurines from the eastern Mediterranean. The discovery of such imported, high-status objects is hardly surprising since by the end of the first millennium BCE India had developed significant overseas trading links.

ABOVE
Ocean-going
ship on a lead
coin of Yajnashri
Satakarni

OPPOSITE
Nashik, Pandu
Lena monastery

These archaeological finds in conjunction with the evidence of the *Periplus* indicate that Indian Ocean contacts impacted on the economy of the Konkan ports and their Deccan hinterland. This seaborne network facilitated trade with East Africa, the Red Sea and the Mediterranean. The most important commodities shipped across the Arabian Sea from all across India were forest products such as spices, like pepper, ginger, cardamom and myrobalan, and timbers, such as ebony, teak and sandalwood. The section of the Western Ghats considered here did not produce spices however. Imports, especially from the eastern Mediterranean via the Red Sea, included wine and to a lesser extent olive oil, together with myrrh, metallic and glass objects, and ceramics and coins. Among the numerous earthenware ceramics are Roman amphorae and Mesopotamian torpedo jars, though Roman products constitute only a small proportion of the ceramics found at Konkan ports in contrast to the higher proportion of Roman ceramics recovered at select ports in the south and east of India.

The burgeoning Arabian Sea trade during this period meant that people and goods had to traverse the valleys and passes of the Western Ghats to access the markets at major population centres in the Deccan heartland. Such commercial movement influenced the location and prosperity of urban settlements. To this day, major cities in Maharashtra such as Pune, Nashik and Kolhapur owe their prosperity to alignments with these long-established trade routes. The rock-cut monasteries described in this volume are the most visible ancient vestiges of these thoroughfares, and the close relationship between the economy and monastic communities is one of the outstanding features of religious life in the Western Ghats during these early centuries.

BUDDHIST COMMUNITIES AND THEIR PATRONS

The rock-cut monasteries of the Western Ghats and the Konkan belong to a period of Indian history marked by significant developments in religion, the state and the economy. Originating in northern India in the 6th-5th centuries BCE, Buddhism spread rapidly throughout much of the country, especially after it was adopted as the official state religion by Ashoka of the Maurya dyasty (r. ca 268-232 BCE), who ruled from his capital of Pataliputra in what is now the state of Bihar. In consequence of

his imperial patronage, Buddhist monasteries for monks and nuns were established at numerous sites across the country.

The *raison d'etre* of the *sangha* then and indeed today is the pursuit of *nirvana,* the state of enlightenment that is beyond the suffering of wordly afflictions such as craving and ignorance. The Buddha had been the first to achieve this goal and the monks and nuns that inhabited rock-cut monasteries followed his path through day-to-day activities like meditation and studying the Buddhist canon. Caves were particularly well suited to this purpose being cool and shady, even in the stifling Indian summer. Evidence from the Western Ghats also points to a more sociable side to monastic life with large open spaces within the caves suitable for communal gatherings that included monastic meetings, meals and ceremonies. Leisure time was also available as dice have been recovered from cracks in the walls and game-boards were etched into *vihara* floors. Monasteries were situated at a distance from settlements to allow their inhabitants to live a detached life of religious focus.

Though Buddhist communities were isolated from general society, the religion enjoyed a broad appeal and considerable interaction with the wider world. The monastic community was after all dependent on the laity for its subsistence as monastic rules prohibited labour. By the end of the first millennium BCE, such interaction led to monasteries becoming wealthy institutions embellished with elaborate architecture accommodating increasingly populous communities. This allowed the religion to expand rapidly from its genesis in northern India to the Deccan, where it gained considerable following."

Stone edict of the Maurya emperor Ashoka discovered at Sopara

Literary references suggest that Buddhism was introduced into the Deccan during the life of the Buddha, prior to the cutting of rock-cut monasteries described in this volume. Among the texts that record this possibly speculative early chronology are the *Parayana Vagga* of the *Suttanipata* and the *Dipavaṃsa*. The *Mahavaṃsa*, another such text, specifically refers to a Buddhist presence at Sopara (some 60 kilometres north of central Mumbai). The discovery of a stone edict of Ashoka at this port site confirms the expansion of the Maurya empire into the western Deccan prior to the first rock-cut monasteries. Inscriptions provide further confirmation of Buddhist affiliations, even though these are no earlier than the 2nd-1st centuries BCE. So far more than 200 such records have been found, all in Prakrit, the standard language of early Indian Buddhism, written in the Brahmi script. Twelve of these mention particular Buddhists sects, like the Bhadrayaniya Dharmottariya and Chetika groups. These early Buddhist groups are often labelled Hinayana or Theravada, although such terms are avoided here: "Hinayana", due to its pejorative associations in later Mahayana scriptures; and "Theravada", because of its common application to Sri Lankan and mainland Southeast Asian Buddhism. The inscriptions also mention the Mahasanghika among other sects linked with the later Mahayana Buddhist tradition.

Information about the economic life of rock-cut monasteries is also found in inscriptions. The presentation of gifts to the Buddhist community known as the *sangha*, was considered the highest mark of honour for the laity. Donations funded cutting into the rock, especially for residential *viharas* and adjacent water cisterns, and sometimes also the costs of food and clothing for monks and nuns. Larger donations took the form of land grants, specifying the villages or fields from which revenues were to accrue, as well as perpetual endowments from investments. Revenues were used for employing laity in essential tasks of financial administration and execution of menial tasks. The subsistence arrangements that physically supported the *sangha* were well regulated and integrated with local rural economic life.

Communications between the *sangha* and the laity were maintained through contributions collected by monks touring settlements that favoured their institutions. Other than during the rainy season, when they were confined to the rock-cut shelters, monks travelled between cities and towns, begging and preaching the

Kanheri, Darbar Hall (Cave 11), interior of dining hall

Buddhist *dharma*, or doctrine. Begging in the Buddhist tradition was not considered charity, since it offered benefits to the giver as well as the receiver. Members of the laity made pilgrimages to the monasteries, not only for personal merit, but also for proclaiming their identity and prestige within wider society. The inscription of a donor's name on an architectural feature placed the presence of the individual in the company of the *sangha* or even an important relic, thereby guaranteeing permanent religious merit. Sponsors were so eager to avail themselves of such merit that they often had their names engraved on the walls of a project before it was finished. This explains the grants made by eleven individuals to the Buddhist community of the Manmodi Hill monastery outside Junnar, recorded in the verandah of the *chaitya* (Cave 26) of the Amba Ambika Group.

Feasts to which the laity were invited were among the most important ceremonies held in the rock-cut monasteries. Such occasions, where the laity interacted with the *sangha*, were subject to strict rules governing seating arrangements, foods served, rituals performed and prayers recited. The larger caves in the monasteries probably functioned as dining halls on such occasions. Cave 11 at Kanheri is even provided with rock-cut benches for monks to sit at. The *uposatha* mentioned in various Buddhist texts of the period was another important ceremony that took place in many of the monasteries. Enacted every two weeks, this observance offered opportunities for the laity to observe and participate in rituals of veneration and gift giving. Shrines known as *chaityas* with focal *stupas* (explained in the following chapter) are likely to have been the main locales of such formalities.

Lay pilgrims travelling along trade routes through the Western Ghats played a crucial role in the life of Buddhist communities. Many visitors seem to have been wealthy merchants coming from settlements named in the inscriptions and that can be identified today. Their diverse and often widespread origins confirm the dissemination of Buddhism throughout the Satavahana dominions and beyond. As already pointed out, a number of donors describe themselves as *yavanas*, but their Indian names testify to a considerable degree of cultural assimilation by this time.

Market traders and craftspeople, sometimes organised into professional guilds, such as blacksmiths, goldsmiths, jewellers, dyers and weavers, also made significant contributions. In this manner, there was ongoing interaction between monks and nuns and local populations. Indeed, the wealth of commercial centres is the best explanation for the sustained sponsorship of some of the monasteries. The occupation of the Kanheri institution, which lasted more than 1,000 years, was thanks to the monastery's strategic location close to successful, Arabian Sea port towns. Merchants and traders were particularly attracted to Buddhism, since the religion offered protection to maritime travel. Carved scenes depicting the Bodhisattva Avalokiteshvara delivering his followers from the Eight Perils, even included shipwreck, as at Kanheri (Cave 90).

ARCHITECTURE AND ART

CUTTING INTO ROCK

CHAITYAS AND VIHARAS

ANIMAL AND FIGURAL CARVINGS

PAINTING

Karla, *Chaitya* (Cave 8), interior

CUTTING INTO ROCK

The method by which the "caves" were excavated out of basalt cliff faces was laborious and deserves explanation. The evidence of the monuments themselves, especially those left unfinished like the *chaitya* hall (Cave 40) of the Bhutling Group on Manmodi Hill outside Junnar, indicates they were fashioned from the top downwards. The first step was to incise an outline of the facade onto the cliff, then work began on cutting deep into the rocky mass to create the interior. This was achieved with only the most rudimentary tools - iron hammers, axes and chisels. The enterprise must have been strictly supervised judging from the vertical walls, horizontal ceilings, curved vaults and column alignments that were sometimes achieved with remarkable precision. Exactly how such perfectly created excavations and their component elements were designed and then realised remains a mystery. Most likely there would have been a team comprising a master architect to conceive and supervise the project; stone-cutters to remove the rock; skilled masons to fashion the architectural components; and specialists responsible for finishing the ornamental details and figural carvings. As for the number of people involved, this remains unknown.

Considerable organisation and planning must have been necessary, with the master architect regularly consulting the sponsor. The monuments were probably worked on for comparatively short periods of time, maybe a few months, with additions and extensions often made later. Evidence from the incomplete caves suggests different teams were employed simultaneously on a project, the finishers often executing facade details when the cutting of interiors had barely commenced. When funds were exhausted and/or the rock was found to be unsuitably soft or damaged by a natural geological fault, the project was entirely abandoned, as in the Bhutling *chaitya* just noted. More commonly, portions were left unfinished, as in the facade of the Kanheri *chaitya*.

Many details of rock-cut monasteries closely resemble structural timber buildings, which were commonplace when the caves were excavated, but which have now disappeared. This is apparent in the halls and verandahs of shrines and residences wherein monolithic pillars and beams give the illusion of "supporting" ceilings and vaults. Columns with octagonal shafts and pot-shaped bases and capitals imitate timber and metallic originals. *Chaitya* arches, either perforated as windows or reproduced in shallow relief to head doorways, have typical horseshoe-

Junnar,
Manmodi Hill,
Bhutling Group,
Chaitya (Cave 40),
facade

shaped profiles derived from curving timbers, most likely achieved with bent bamboos. Timber-like ribs and rafters within the arches affirm their wooden origins. Rock-cut facades are often conceived as multi-storeyed architectural compositions, complete with timber-like railings and balconies carried on projecting brackets. Genuine wooden elements are sometimes introduced, as if to reproduce an actual timber shrine or dwelling. Examples are the remnants of a teak screen inside the arched window of the Kondane *chaitya*, and the teak ribs and rafters inserted into the curved vaults of the Karla and Bhaja *chaityas*. Such literal uses of wood are sometimes considered indicative of the earliest excavations, to be replaced over time by stone imitations.

Bedsa, *Chaitya* (Cave 7), interior *stupa*

CHAITYAS AND VIHARAS

In form and function, the two main categories of rock-cut caves in Buddhist monasteries are shrines for the rites of worship, known as *chaityas*, and residences with sleeping cells for monks or nuns, generally known as *viharas*. Though varying in shape and scale, *chaityas* are characterised by *stupas* (generally termed *dagobas* in the Pali language of ancient Buddhist texts) that served as a devotional focus for monks and nuns, as well as for visiting laity. *Stupas* were the preferred architectural receptacle for holy relics commemorating the Master and his followers, though some *stupas* were used to honour the deaths of pious individuals, whose names were inscribed on their cylindrical bases. Such memorials are usually clustered in groups, as in the rock-cut *stupas* in Cave 20 at Bhaja. In later times, *stupas* often had a broader significance since they came to represent the Buddhist *dharma* itself.

As *stupas* developed, their hemispherical "domes" were raised on ever-higher cylindrical drums, and they came to be surrounded by posts and railings that defined a path around the circular base, which devotees proceeded along in a clockwise direction, a dynamic of veneration known as *pradakshina*. At the top of the dome were tiny representations of square, post-and-railing enclosures known as *harmikas*, framing an inverted, stepped abacus above. (This latter term is borrowed from European Classical architecture, where it refers to the support of a column capital, a usage generally applied to column capitals in early Indian architecture.) Crowning the dome was the *chhatra*, an umbrella-like finial, sometimes heightened with multiple, superimposed tiers. Rock-cut *stupas* reproduce all these components in monolithic form, with the crowning *chhatra* occasionally fashioned out of actual timbers, as in the Karla *chaitya*, or carved onto the stone ceiling above.

The grandest *chaityas* in the monasteries of the Western Ghats are those with a long hall divided by two lines of columns into a central nave flanked by side aisles, the latter curving behind the focal *stupa*. This semicircular-ended plan allowed worshippers to proceed towards the *stupa* along the passage created by the pillars, and then to pass around the *stupa* as part of the *pradakshina* rite. The nave is invariably roofed with a lofty arched vault that emerges on the outer facade as a great horseshoe-shaped *chaitya* arch or window; hence the somewhat confusing terminological overlap between the hall itself and its frontal arched window.

As already mentioned, the vaults of *chaitya* halls are sometimes lined with timber ribs in imitation of free-standing wooden architecture. Notches where these ribs have been lost can still be seen, as in the *chaitya* (Cave 3) at Kanheri. Timbers are, on occasion, also used to close off the frontal *chaitya* window by creating a screen with curving ribs to filter the light, fragments of which are preserved at Karla and Kondane. Timber-like stone ribs set into the curving sides of the window openings often accompany such actual wooden elements. The columns supporting the vaults of the earliest *chaitya* halls, like that at Bhaja, lean inwards slightly, as if to resist the outward thrust of an actual timber vault, a feature that disappears in later *chaityas* where the columns are truly vertical.

In larger *chaityas* a wall is introduced to separate the interior of the hall from its exterior facade. Smaller but similar *chaitya* arches, in shallow relief rather than as windows, head the doorways in this wall. This juxtaposition of smaller, lesser *chaitya* arches in relief, often filled with decorative designs in imitation of actual timber screens, with the greater, *chaitya* window above, results in imposing facade compositions, like those of Pandu Lena (Cave 18) and Manmodi (Cave 40) outside Junnar. In some cases, doorways are preceded by a verandah flanked by architectural compositions in relief, and on occasion by majestic elephant torsos, as at Karla. Sometimes stone screens and lofty monolithic columns partly conceal the façade from external view.

The scheme just described represents the fully developed *chaitya* in early Buddhist rock-cut architecture. However there are significant variants, notably the circular *chaitya* with a dome-like ceiling and a *stupa* in the middle surrounded by a ring of columns. The example at Tulja Lena outside Junnar (Cave 3) is considered by some scholars to be one of the earliest excavations in the Western Ghats due to its resemblance to the circular, rock-cut shrine in the Barabar caves in Bihar, which dates from the 3rd century BCE. The *chaitya* at Mahakala (Kondivte) (Cave 9), another small circular shrine though without columns, is also accorded an early date. Lesser, more commonly occurring *chaityas* are those with square or rectangular flat-roofed interiors accommodating a *stupa* at one end, such as those around Junnar (Shivneri Cave 43) and at Kuda (Cave 6). Like their semicircular-ended counterparts, these too are entered through doorways set within a columned verandah. Many *chaityas* at Kanheri dispense with the focal *stupa*, replacing it with a small chamber cut into the rear wall to accommodate an enthroned Buddha flanked by Bodhisattvas.

Residential *viharas* are an essential component of all rock-cut monastic establishments. While inscriptions found in these excavations sometimes refer to such residences as *mantaps* (*mandapas*), the more widely accepted term for a Buddhist habitation, *vihara*, is employed here. Of the more than 500 Buddhist caves in the Western Ghats, more than 80 per cent are *viharas*. The most well known type has a square or rectangular flat-roofed hall with small cells cut into the rear and side walls, and an entrance on the fourth, frontal side. Fine examples of such *viharas* include those at Pandu Lena (Caves 3 and 10), Junnar (Lenyadri Cave 7) and Kondane (Cave 2). The cells are often provided with rock-cut beds, lamp alcoves, and sockets to anchor poles for hanging robes, all

Karla, *Chaitya* (Cave 8), plan and section

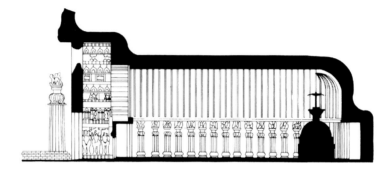

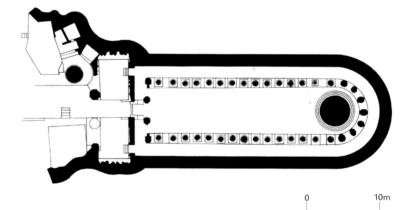

0   10m

ARCHITECTURE AND ART

of which offer an insight into the private living conditions of monks and nuns. In contrast, the central halls attest to the more sociable aspects of monastic life. A development in the architecture of *viharas* that indicates a later phase in monastic life is the introduction of a shrine for worship set into the rear walls. At first this was probably achieved through a relief representation of a *stupa*, as in Pandu Lena (Cave 3). Later, the shrine was expanded to accommodate a sculpted preaching Buddha, usually accompanied by Bodhisattvas, preceded by a small vestibule. Numerous examples of such *vihara*-shrines are found at Kanheri.

Not all *viharas* conform to the schemes just described. An exception is Cave 11 at Bedsa, which imitates the semicircular-ended layout of a *chaitya* hall, but with cells cut into the side and curving walls. In more elaborate *viharas*, including the Bedsa example, cell doorways are headed by fully modelled *chaitya* arches set between friezes of imitation facades. Low benches for seating set into the side walls indicate that the caves were also used as places of assembly and perhaps also of prayer. In one unique *vihara* at Kanheri (Cave 11) two low benches are cut out of the floor, most likely for monks to sit when studying and reciting sacred texts. Larger *viharas* are preceded by a verandah with one or more doorways. Some have perforated windows to admit light. It should also be noted that most *viharas* include only a few cells and no central hall, indicating the solitary nature of monastic life.

Nashik, Pandu Lena, plans of *viharas* (Caves 3 and 10)

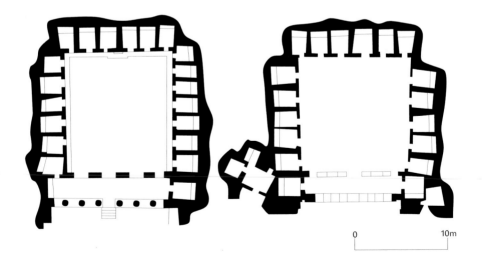

0   10m

Ubiquitous amongst *viharas* are the rock-cut water cisterns on which monastic life depended, usually cut out of the cliffs next to cave entrances. Cisterns that filled with rainwater during the monsoon continued to provide water for monks and nuns throughout the dry seasons that followed. At Kanheri there is evidence of an ingenious hydraulic system that trapped and stored water, to be conveyed via rock-cut channels to the numerous *viharas* scattered across this extensive site.

Kanheri, rock-cut cistern

The elements of rock-cut monasteries that receive the greatest architectural attention are columns and windows. Columns in the verandahs of halls and shrines, and lining the central naves of *chaityas*, are often provided with pot-like bases, octagonal shafts, and inverted-pot or lotus petalled capitals. Capitals can be capped with two-part abacuses consisting of diminutive ribbed *amalakas*, often set in box-like frames, and inverted, stepped-pyramidal motifs (similar to those on top of *stupas*). The most beautiful brackets were fashioned as paired animals with human riders (described below). Where verandahs are provided with balconies with imitation posts and railings, the bases of the columns are concealed. The earlier history of the designs is evident from the lofty columns in front of the Karla and Kanheri *chaityas* (Caves 8, and 3,

ABOVE
Nashik, Pandu Lena, *Chaitya* (Cave 18), window

OPPOSITE
Bedsa, *Chaitya* (Cave 7), verandah columns and façade

respectively). These monolithic pillars resemble the free-standing columns erected by Ashoka as part of his policy of promoting Buddhism throughout the Maurya empire. The Karla column shares with these 3rd-century BCE prototypes the same lotus-petalled capital crowned with quartets of lions.

Chaitya arches with horseshoe-shaped profiles are arguably the most distinctive attribute of rock-cut monasteries, whether as windows dominating *chaitya* facades, or as smaller "blind" windows heading doorways or incorporated into shallow-relief multi-storeyed facades. Whatever their scale or application, the arches are consistent in shape, with identical frames incorporating side wings and capping finials, presumably reproducing wooden templates. Notches in some examples suggest that arches may have been faced with actual timbers. The curving ribbed screens within, either in wood or in shallow relief in stone, have already been noted.

ANIMAL AND FIGURAL CARVINGS

Most of the caves in the monasteries described in this volume were completed by the 2nd-3rd centuries CE. This was before carved and painted images of the Buddha started to embellish Buddhist monuments in northern and central India and the monastic shrines and residences in the Western Ghats. Visitors should remember that the carvings of the Buddha and of the Buddhist saviours known as Bodhisattvas seen in many of the caves are all later additions. In the earlier period, the principal events in the life of the Master, together with his death, were indicated by symbols linked with specific locales: notably the *bodhi* tree under which Buddha attained enlightenment at Bodhgaya; the *dharmachakra*, the spoked wheel indicating the "turning of the law" sermon that he preached at Sarnath; and the *stupa*, referring to the funerary monument at Kusinagara, in which his ashes were interred after he was cremated. Such potent Buddhist motifs appear occasionally, as over the doorway of Cave 3 in Pandu Lena, but are not usually accorded particular prominence.

The sculptural themes contemporary with the early excavations depict men, women and animals from everyday life of the society that supported the monks and nuns. Among the most appealing subjects are human couples riding on pairs of crouching elephants, tigers, lions, bulls, horses and winged fantastic beasts. These appear as bracket figures surmounting columns in the verandahs of *chaityas*, as in Pandu Lena (Caves 10 and 17), and, most spectacularly, in the *chaitya* halls at Karla, Bedsa and Kanheri. Here, men and women are sculpted in a convincing lifelike manner, often with one hand held up as if greeting visitors. Such couples are also shown peering out of windows in architectural facades, most notably at Bhaja and Kondane, giving the impression of multi-storeyed palaces populated by welcoming inhabitants.

Male and female couples depicted in a variety of affectionate embraces, known as *mithunas*, are a related theme, best seen in the verandahs of the Karla and Kanheri *chaityas*. In some compositions, the figures are depicted as dancers, as in the relief architectural facades at Karla and Kondane. Fully modelled to display their bare and fleshy torsos, clad in gorgeous jewellery and with elaborate hairdos, these men and women can never have been intended as portraits of Buddhist teachers, monks or nuns, nor of the donors who contributed to the costs of cutting the monuments, though this has occasionally been suggested.

On the contrary, these couples are best understood as propitious figures protecting the sacred monument. (Such auspicious couples are not unique to early Buddhist art, as is demonstrated by the *mithunas* in the verandahs and entrance porches of later Hindu temples.)

    Depictions of human devotees are rare in Buddhist monastic art in the Western Ghats, an exception being the courtly maidens venerating the *stupa* carved in relief onto the rear wall of the "queen's cave" at Pandu Lena (Cave 3). More usually, devotees take the form of semi-divine creatures, like *nagas* with serpent hoods, who guard the treasures of the underworld, and *yakshas* and *yakshis*, the semi-divine male and female spirits who embody the powers of nature. In the Pandu Lena cave, *yakshas* with characteristic protruding bellies are sculpted as if emerging out of the ground to support the frontal verandah. Another popular deity is Lakshmi, the goddess personifying good fortune and wealth, often accompanied by elephants. She appears as the central figure in the relief composition heading the doorway to the Bhutling *chaitya* (Cave 40).

Karla, *Chaitya* (Cave 8), *mithuna* couples and later Bodhisattva image in the verandah

ARCHITECTURE AND ART

The figural art in the monasteries very occasionally incorporates narratives, in contrast to structural *stupas* at other Buddhist sites such as Sanchi in central India, or Amaravati and Nagarjunakonda in the Andhra zone of the eastern Deccan. However, where they do occur, as in the tiny panels around the doorway of Cave 3 at Pandu Lena, the narrative has usually not been identified. This is the case with the considerably larger wall compositions in the verandah of Cave 22 at Bhaja, which portray figures in a horse-drawn chariot and riding a richly caparisoned elephant flying through the sky. Confident identification of these scenes has so far eluded scholars, despite the obvious military character of these figures as well as the armed guards carved onto the adjacent walls. A royal quality is also evident in the animal art of many caves, as in the lions that surmount the enormous monolithic columns in front of the Karla and Kanheri *chaityas*. As already mentioned, these imitate the animal capitals of Ashoka's imperial pillars. The great elephants carved with convincing naturalism in almost three dimensions on the side walls of the verandah in the Karla *chaitya* are no less regal.

Later developments in the Buddhist religion of northern India starting in the 4th-5th centuries had an impact on the sculptural art of those monasteries in the Western Ghats that flourished during this period, notably Karla, Kanheri and Kuda, which were furnished with Buddha and Bodhisattva figures. This "intrusive" imagery reflected changes in the devotional practices of monks, nuns and lay people, which now required icons of the Master and of Bodhisattvas and which may have been related to the dispersal of Mahayana doctrine through the Deccan. Some *chaityas* excavated during these later centuries, such as in Cave 90 at Kanheri, have a chamber cut into the rear wall to accommodate a separately sculpted Buddha figure. There must also have been changes in the organisation of the *sangha*, though there is little evidence of this in the layouts of the caves.

Compared with the naturalism and expressive gestures of the *mithunas*, later Buddhist figures are more conventional, though noteworthy for their serene poise and introspection. Representations of Buddha portray the Master seated on an open lotus flower, his feet folded up in meditation, or placed firmly on the ground, his hands brought together in the gestures of preaching the doctrine (*dharmachakra-mudra*) or offering blessings (*varada-mudra*). It is in these two roles of preaching and blessing that Buddha is most frequently

Bhaja, Cave 22, verandah wall panel depicting riders in a chariot trampling a writhing demon

ABOVE
Kanheri, Cave
90, seated
and standing
Buddhas with
attendants

OPPOSITE
Kanheri, Cave
34, ceiling
painting of
seated Buddha

encountered in later monastic art, sometimes carved onto the base of a *stupa*, on other occasions set into a recess in the rear wall of *chaityas*, or, more commonly, in multiple, identical images, both large and small, covering the walls of verandahs and halls of *chaityas* and *viharas*. This repetitive imagery suggests that donors may have financed individual figures, though no records of such commissions are available. As is usual in this later iconography, the Buddha is accompanied by saviour figures known as Bodhisattvas, who intercede with the Master on behalf of devotees. The Bodhisattva most often depicted is Avalokiteshvara, also known as Padmapani, Lord of the Lotus, from the prominent blossom with a trailing stalk that he holds in the right hand. That Avalokiteshvara's primary mission is salvation is graphically illustrated in sculpted scenes in Caves 2 and 90 at Kanheri, where his followers are being rescued from a variety of vividly illustrated perils.

One explanation for standardised Buddhist imagery in the rock-cut monasteries is that this figural art was already fully developed elsewhere in the Deccan by the time it came to be imported to the Western Ghats, presumably by itinerant master artists seeking work. The most likely sources of this tradition are Amaravati and Nagarjunakonda, where the Ikshvakus, successors to the Satavahanas, sponsored structural monasteries in the 3rd-4th centuries, and Ajanta, where the Vakatakas and others expanded and elaborated the rock-cut site in the late 5th century. In accordance with this well-established art tradition, Buddhas and Bodhisattvas in the Karla and Kanheri monasteries are clad in diaphanous long garments that reveal the smooth modelling of their bodies. The faces have sharply pointed noses and the ears have long lobes; the hair is arranged in small curls, with a characteristic topknot; and the typical hand gestures are of preaching and blessing. For the most part these figures are small, though the gravity of preaching Buddhas is sometimes emphasised by the lotuses on which they are seated, the blossom being raised on a cylindrical stalk held by *nagas* and gods. The standing Buddhas in the verandah of the Kanheri *chaitya* have a colossal height of more than 7 metres, making them the largest such figures in all Deccan Buddhist sculpture, matched only by the "sleeping" Buddha of similar dimensions in Cave 26 in Ajanta.

PAINTING

As at Ajanta, the walls and ceilings of some caves of the Western Ghats were probably covered with paintings on a plaster base, either shortly after they were excavated, or as they continued to be used in later centuries. But only in Cave 34 at Kanheri can an unfinished composition portraying the seated Buddha now be seen. Floral and geometric designs must also have been popular, but again there are only the barest traces of such schemes, as on the ceiling of Cave 48 on Shivneri near Junnar. These two remnants give tantalising hints of a vanished pictorial tradition.

OUTSIDE NASHIK

PANDU LENA

Nashik, Pandu Lena, Cave 10, view

Known in ancient times as Mount Trirashmi, Pandu Lena outside Nashik comprises a series of 24 excavations strung for some 300 metres along an escarpment that forms an outlying ridge of the Western Ghats. Located just off National Highway 3, some 9 kilometres south of Nashik city, the caves face north on to a trade route that led through Thal Ghat, the mountain pass to the west. While the caves display the same constituent components found at other rock-cut sites in the region, at Pandu Lena they are more substantial and often excavated with greater skill. Doorways, for instance, are larger than elsewhere and are particularly well fashioned. The precision and size of the letters in the inscriptions betray the work of highly proficient artisans.

Remains of an ancient settlement at Nashik can still be seen in the form of a high mound close to the *ghats* and temples on the south bank of the Godavari that flows through the middle of the modern city. The mound attests to the enduring religious importance of Nashik being on one of India's holiest rivers. In ancient times Nashik was located in the northwestern part of the Satavahana kingdom. Being close to the border between the Satavahanas and their adversaries the Kshatrapas, Nashik held great strategic importance, resulting in significant expansion of the monastery during the 1st-2nd centuries CE with the addition of exquisitely carved caves.

Of all the monasteries in the Western Ghats, evidence from Pandu Lena can help to reconstruct contemporary political events, notably the conflict between the two ancient dynasties that contested this part of the Deccan. Inscriptions in Caves 3 and 10, for instance, record support for the monastery both by Nahapana, the Kshatrapa king, and his adversary Gautamiputra Satakarni, the Satavahana king. Gautamiputra is known to have defeated Nahapana in the early 1st century CE, thereby bringing to an end Kshatrapa control of the strategic routes through the Western Ghats, and re-establishing Satavahana supremacy in the region. Donations by these and other figures record funds to cover the costs of the excavations, and provide income from land grants for the expenses of the religious ceremonies and everyday lives of the monks and nuns. The homes of the sponsors mentioned indicate the long distances that these royal figures or their representatives travelled in order to visit the site. There is even a notice of a *yavana* sponsor in Cave 17.

See photographs on pages 16 and 17

The Pandu Lena excavations are situated in close proximity to one another and would have formed a coherent complex, with monks and nuns living in individual caves but making everyday contact. The monastery has a long history, beginning in the 2nd-1st century BCE with Cave 19, which bears an inscription dating its excavation to the reign of one of the earliest known Satavahana monarchs. Final activity at Nashik, as represented by the Buddha figures in the first and last caves of the site, may be assigned to the 5th-6th centuries. Although this chronology indicates an expansion of Pandu Lena over more than six centuries, there is little evidence of activity during the 3rd-4th centuries.

PANDU LENA

The Pandu Lena caves are approached via a long path, with steps to the middle of the excavations, numbered from right to left (west to east). Visitors should begin their tour at Cave 2, at the extreme west or right end of the site if facing the scarp. Judging from the worn railing motif on the cliff above, this may have been an early excavation. If so, it was altogether reworked in the 5th-6th centuries, when carvings of preaching Buddhas seated in the company of attendants holding fly-whisks were added. Figures in one composition have their feet firmly placed on open lotus flowers.

Pandu Lena,
Caves 1 and 2

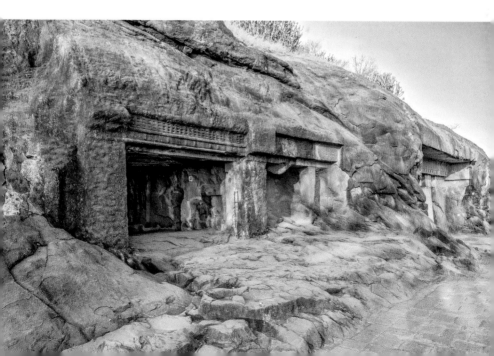

Pandu Lena,
Cave 3, verandah
doorway
See also
photograph
of exterior on
page 17 and
illustration on
page 34

Cave 3, the next excavation, is one of the largest and most elaborate early *viharas* of the Pandu Lena monastery. The six octagonal columns of its outer verandah have cushion-shaped capitals with two-part abacuses comprising tiny *amalakas* and larger, inverted-stepped pyramids. These support brackets sculpted in the form of seated elephants, bulls and fantastic beasts, all with human riders, which in turn carry a lintel imitating timber construction. The balcony walls concealing the column bases are also treated as if made of timber. They appear to be supported by *yakshas* with grimacing faces, each with one hand held up, the lower body concealed as if emerging from out of the rock beneath. Imitation rafters and railings adorn the ceiling inside. The doorway in the verandah leading to the hall within is set within a shallow relief representation of a wooden *torana*, with a pair of posts decorated with panels filled with tiny male and female figures, in what appear to be scenes from two stories ending in the rescue and abduction of a woman. Some interpreters have suggested that the scenes illustrate the stories of the chaste and unchaste woman, but one scholar postulates that they depict contemporary historical events, being linked with Gautamiputra and his wife. Whatever, they are unique in the Buddhist art of the Western Ghats. The posts of the *torana* support two lintels: the lower one with rampant *yalis*; the upper one with spiral ends. Panels in between show the worshippers venerating the *bodhi* tree, *stupa* and *dharmachakra*. Guardians with fleshy bodies, each carrying a bunch of flowers in one hand, the other hand firmly placed on the hip, are carved at either side of the *torana*. Inscribed panels on the verandah walls include a grant by the Satavahana queen Gautama Balashri.

Pandu Lena, Cave 3, *stupa panel inside the hall*

The almost square hall of Cave 3, measuring 12 by 14 metres, has eighteen small cells with rock-cut beds, with two more accessed through the verandah. In the middle of the rear wall is a panel embellished with a relief *stupa* topped by an inverted stepped abacus, from which sprout five *chhatra* finials, adored by courtly maidens. The maiden on the left has her hands brought together in a gesture of veneration; a small lion torso and a flying celestial are seen above. On the right, the maiden holds a fly-whisk, and is surmounted by a *dharmachakra* and another celestial. These figures seem appropriate for a monument, referred to in one inscription as Devi Lena, or Queen's Cave.

The next excavation of Pandu Lena to be described here is Cave 10, a well-preserved *vihara* imitating many features of Cave 3. There is, however, no balcony, the six columns of its verandah being fully exposed, from their pot-shaped bases to the clearly carved animal brackets above. There are six inscriptions in Cave 10, some with large letters like those on the verandah wall mentioning the Kshatrapa king Nahapana and his son-in-law Ushavadata. One of these mentions a land grant in the 42nd year of Nahapana's reign (ca 148 CE). The hall, which is accessed through three doorways in the verandah, is generous in size, measuring no less than 11 by 14 metres. It is surrounded by sixteen cells

See photographs on pages 16 and 44-45, and illustration on page 34

Pandu Lena,
Chaitya
(Cave 18)

RIGHT
Doorway with
guardian figure
OPPOSITE
Interior of hall
with *stupa*

*See also
photographs on
pages 1 and 36*

with a panel in the middle of the rear wall. This has a crudely modelled
guardian figure armed with a club, carved over an earlier relief *stupa*,
presumably like that in Cave 3, of which the *harmika*, abacus and triple
chhatras can still be made out.

The *Chaitya* (Cave 18) of the Pandu Lena monastery dates back to
the 2nd-1st century BCE and is notable for its richly adorned, well-preserved
façade. A typical *chaitya* arch in relief surmounts the central doorway to the
hall. On the left of the central doorway is a male guardian holding a bunch
of flowers. If there was a similar figure on the right, this has been lost. A
chaitya arch in relief surmounts the doorway. This contains a semicircle
filled with a petalled lattice, above which sits a lunette filled with curving
ribs with tendril-like ends containing minute elephants, horses and bulls.
Over this arch rises a similarly shaped, much larger *chaitya* window with
articulated timber-like ribs inside the opening. This forms the centrepiece
of an elaborate composition in shallow relief incorporating posts and
railings, and columns with bell-shaped capitals and animal brackets
alternating with *stupas*, topped by a line of four larger *chaitya* arches.

One inscription on Cave 18 mentions that the "chetiya-gharam" was a gift of a woman who was both the daughter of a royal minister and the wife of another. Evidently a person of some influence and wealth, she could surely have provided sufficient funds to complete the *chaitya*. However, the excavation was a collaborative endeavour since two other records indicate that citizens of "Nasika" financed certain portions of the façade decoration.

The interior of Cave 18 is almost 12 metres deep and 7 metres wide. Its central nave is lined with slender octagonal columns, ten with pot-shaped bases. Holes in the cornice above indicate the positions of timbers, presumably curving ribs to create the illusion of a wooden vault, now vanished. The focal monolithic *stupa* has a notably high drum crowned with a small railing. The *harmika* has the usual inverted-stepped pyramidal abacus, but no *chhatra*.

Cave 17 is a *vihara* adjacent to the upper portion of Cave 18, reached by a flight of steps to the right of the *chaitya*. The *vihara* has a verandah with columns of the same type as Caves 3 and 10, but here there are only four rather than six supports. An inscription on its rear wall records that the *vihara* was donated by Indragnimitra, who "adhered to the *dharma*" for the benefit of the community of the "four directions". This donor identifies himself as a *yavana* from Damtamiti, sometimes identified with a town that flourished in the 1st-2nd centuries CE in the Hellenised Bactrian kingdom of eastern Afghanistan.

In spite of Indragnimitra's bequest, the interior of Cave 17 was never completed. A plain doorway leads into an unsymmetrical and unfinished hall with four cells opening off to one side only, and a chamber for worship cut into the rear wall. A line of four columns (the square shafts are restorations) with animal brackets creates a transverse verandah at the back, perhaps intended to separate the residential section of the hall from the chamber for worship. Its left wall has a long recess possibly intended for a row of separately sculpted Buddha images to be added in later times. Even so, the central chamber was left as an uncut mass, presumably for a *stupa*, either in three dimensions, or engraved in relief on its back wall.

A flight of steps to the left of the *chaitya* (Cave 18) leads to Cave 20. Though excavated during the early Satavahana era, this *vihara* was also embellished in later times, when images of the preaching

Pandu Lena, Cave 17, view

Buddha and tall Bodhisattvas with attendant females were added to its rear shrine. The six verandah columns with pot-like bases, however, are original features, as are the fifteen cells cut into the side walls of the spacious hall, more than 18 metres deep and 12 metres wide. Cave 19, immediately beneath Cave 20, is a small *vihara* with perforated windows in the verandah, and decorated railings and arches over the cell doorways inside the hall. Samana, an envoy of the early Satavahana king Krishna, is the author of an inscription carved on to the rear wall of the verandah.

Visitors should continue to the end of Pandu Lena site to inspect the carvings in the line of chambers that constitute Caves 23 and 24. Like those already noted in Cave 2, these are additions of the 5th-6th centuries. Most impressive are representations of the Master, depicted larger than life, meditating or preaching, with feet folded up or placed on the ground. The deep modelling of the bodies and the tranquil expressions of the faces rank these images among the finest achievements in Deccan Buddhist art, comparable to broadly contemporary sculptures at Ajanta and Ellora.

BELOW
Pandu Lena,
Cave 20, interior

OPPOSITE
Pandu Lena,
Buddha figures
in Cave 23

AROUND JUNNAR

TULJA LENA

SHIVNERI

MANMODI HILL
Bhutling
Amba Ambika
Bhimshankar Group

LENYADRI

Manmodi Hill, Bhimshankar Group,
Chaitya (Cave 2), view from beneath

The city of Junnar is attractively situated on the fertile banks of the Kukdi river, dramatically framed by outlying lineaments of the Western Ghats. The Buddhist rock-cut monasteries excavated in four separate groups on the steep faces of the surrounding hills constitute by far the largest concentration of such monuments to be found anywhere in the Deccan. These monasteries probably functioned as independent religious institutions even though the distances between them are by no means great. While each monastery has its own individual chronology, activity in the Junnar area may be assigned to the period spanning the 2nd-1st century BCE to the early 3rd century CE, with little evidence to suggest later occupation or expansion.

Rock-cut monastic sites around Junnar

Archaeological excavations of the substantial ancient mounds along the banks of the Kudki river attest to the existence of a populous and prosperous city although the name by which the city was known at that time is yet to be established. In ancient times the inhabitants of this city would have supported the monastic communities living in the numerous caves found throughout the surrounding hills through gifts of food and funds. Indeed, the location of Junnar, some 30 kilometres east of Nana Ghat, one of the critical mountain passes that linked the Konkan ports and cities like Kalyan with inland Deccan centres like Ter and Paithan, explains its importance during this early period. It is worth noting that at a height of some 750 metres above sea level, Nana Ghat was, in part, artificially cut to create a narrow steep path between high cliffs. The pass derives the name Nana, which translates from Marathi as "coin", from the tolls exacted here from travelling merchants. The strategic importance of the Nana Ghat was recognized by the Satavahana rulers as early as the 2nd century BCE, who had a cave excavated at the head of the pass, furnished with inscribed proclamations and even royal portraits (the latter now obliterated). In contrast, there is among the many inscriptions in the caves around Junnar hardly any mention of a king, queen or representative from the royal families that governed this part of the Deccan. The sole exception is found in Cave 7 of the Bhimshankar Group on Manmodi Hill, which was a donation by a minister of the Kshatrapa king Nahapana.

See photograph on page 15

Of the almost 200 caves cut into the sides of the hills around Junnar only those of greatest architectural and historical interest and which can be easily accessed by following pathways are described here. Visitors must be warned that these routes are often steep and rarely adequately signposted. A tour of the Junnar monasteries is an adventurous excursion and a guide, if one can be found, is recommended. The caves that can now only be reached by experienced rock climbers are not described, though we may speculate as to how monks and nuns in ancient times would have accessed these now unapproachable shrines and residences. Presumably, wooden ladders and walkways must have been used, but these have long ago disappeared.

ABOVE
Tulja Lena,
panorama

OPPOSITE
Tulja Lena,
Chaitya (Cave 3)

TULJA LENA

The first of the monasteries around Junnar to be described is situated 4.5 kilometres west of the city, on the eastern flank of a hill that faces the Kudki valley. Tulja Lena consists of eighteen numbered excavations, disposed in a line along a narrow path beneath a rocky overhang. The only one of architectural importance, Cave 3, is a circular *chaitya*, almost 8 metres in diameter. This contains a central monolithic *stupa* raised on a plain drum, surrounded by twelve slender octagonal columns, without bases or capitals, but with notches cut into the tops of the shafts of the front two columns. The columns support a dome-like roof, now damaged, and impressions of timber ribs suggest a wooden structure once adorned the roof. Nothing remains of the cave's doorway or entrance porch, presumably collapsed. The unique form of the *chaitya* and the highly polished walls of the adjoining cave have suggested to some scholars a date of 2nd-1st century BCE, making it perhaps the first of the Junnar series.

Further evidence for an early date for the Tulja Lena monastery is the adjacent Cave 2. This is a *vihara* with cubical cells, devoid of sleeping

TULJA LENA

benches, opening off a hall measuring some 5.5 metres square. As in Cave 3, nothing remains of its entrance door or porch. Though devoid of ornamentation, the floor and roof of the hall retain traces of slight polish, a technique often found in early examples of Indian architecture, notably the imperial columns of Ashoka, the 3rd-century BCE emperor, and the caves of the same date at Barabar in Bihar.

Caves 4 to 16 are all single-cell excavations of different sizes. Though badly damaged, they preserve fragmentary facades with doorways topped by *chaitya* arches set between relief architectural facades with posts and railings, and lesser arches of the same type. Cave 4, the deepest of the series, serves today as a shrine to Tulaja Bhavani, the popular Hindu goddess after whom the site as a whole takes its name.

SHIVNERI

Celebrated as the birthplace of Shivaji, the great Maratha warrior, Shivneri is a dramatic, triangular shaped basalt outcrop with steep sides rising more than 100 metres above the plain, 3 kilometres south of Junnar. Fortifications protecting the hill on the south, dating mostly from the 15th-16th centuries, are joined by cross walls to create a sequence of gateways that lines the approach road ascending to the flat-topped summit. The interior of the fort is home to a goddess temple commemorating the spot where Jijabai, Shivaji's mother, is believed to have worshipped.

The Buddhist caves of Shivneri are clustered in six separate groups hewn around the sides of the hill at successively higher levels, numbered in a continuous sequence from 1 to 48. However, the only excavations accessible to general visitors are those on the southern flank, of which three merit attention.

Caves 42 and 43 once shared a verandah, but this has now collapsed. Cave 42 is a rectangular, flat-roofed *chaitya* with a bench cut into the rear wall. A relief stupa panel on the wall is now painted red and venerated as a manifestation of a Hindu goddess! Cave 43, another *chaitya*, has a narrow flat-roofed chamber with a well-preserved *stupa*, some 3 metres in diameter, its *harmika* is linked to the *chhatra* carved onto the ceiling. An inscription in the damaged verandah records that the "chettiyaghara" (*chaitya*) was a donation of Virasena, chief of the "gahapatis" (householders), "made for the good and pleasures of the world".

Another flat-roofed *chaitya* higher up along the path is Cave 48. Its stupa has a *harmika* and the usual *chhatra* cut out of the ceiling above. Traces of paint on the ceiling reveal a design of multiple squares filled with different coloured circles.

Manmodi Hill, Bhutling Group, *Chaitya* (Cave 40)

See also photograph on page 29

MANMODI HILL

The largest number of rock-cut monuments around Junnar are hewn into the sides of Manmodi Hill, ancient Manamukuda, some 2 kilometres southeast of the city. The caves are situated over a section of the hill more than 1,500 metres in length, approximately halfway up its height, and are divided into three clusters. The tour recommended here begins on the western part of the hill with the Bhutling Group, which can be accessed on foot from the base of Shivneri hill. The Amba Ambika monastery lies several kilometres to the east of the Bhutling Group, with the Bhimshankar Group several kilometres further still. Motorised transport is therefore recommended for these latter monasteries, which can drop the visitor at the bottom of the steep paths that climb from the base of the hill to each monastery.

Several hundred metres east of Shivneri hill described above is the Bhutling Group, the first series of excavations on Manmodi Hill to be described here. The *Chaitya* (Cave 40) here is by far the most splendid of all the Manmodi monuments. In spite of its unfinished condition, the *chaitya* arch above the broken doorway is well preserved and complete with internal ribs. The arch contains a part-circular panel designed like an ornamental lotus, divided into seven radiating, petal-shaped shallow compartments. The central compartment accommodates a tiny female figure with one arm raised in a gesture of assurance, usually identified as the goddess Lakshmi. Arrayed in symmetrical fashion at either side are elephants standing on lotus flowers holding upside-down pots of water in their trunks; the remaining petals carry tiny male figures, their hands held together over their heads in attitudes of devotion. A short inscription from the 2nd century CE on the *chaitya* window above states that the facade of the hall was the meritorious gift of a *yavana* named Chandra.

Manmodi Hill,
Bhutling Group,
Cave 45

The curving profile of the *chaitya* window dominating the facade of Cave 40 terminates in a tip with a narrow finial. Semi-divine, male figures in deep relief flank the window; one is a winged being, the other is a *naga* deity with serpent hoods. *Stupas* with fully-expressed domes are seen at either side. A band with *chaitya* arches in relief frames the facade, but only the upper portion is preserved. The side walls of the facade are now much eroded. Visitors are recommended not to enter the cave, due to the profusion of bees nests over the entrance. Those who do will notice that work on its interior proceeded from top to bottom,

Manmodi Hill, Amba Ambika Group, *Chaitya* (Cave 26)

but was abandoned when the rock was found to be unsuitably soft. While the hall was obviously intended to have a semicircular-ended nave flanked by octagonal pillars, these supports were only roughly shaped; the vaulted ceiling and the focal *stupa* too remain unfinished.

A short distance from the *chaitya* is a flight of steps climbing up to Cave 45. This comprises a line of four rectangular cells that once shared a common verandah, which has now collapsed. *Chaitya* arches in relief above the doorways have representations of radiating wooden ribs set within a frieze of model *stupas*.

The most impressive monument of the Amba Ambika Group is the *Chaitya* (Cave 26). Its unfinished condition is explained by the occurrence of bands of softer rock from which water percolates. The hall is approached through a verandah with four columns with pot-shaped bases and tops, octagonal shafts, and capitals with inverted-pyramidal abacuses (partly restored). A window that is part-elliptical, rather than the usual *chaitya* horseshoe shape surmounts the doorway inside the verandah. Eleven inscriptions here, dating from the early 2nd century CE, specify gifts of land by various individuals and guilds of craftsmen, as well as funds remitted from interest payments, all in favour of the Amba Ambika monastic community. In spite of this collaborative financial support, the hall was abandoned before the *stupa* could be cut from the

Manmodi Hill, Bhimshankar Group, *Chaitya* (Cave 2), interior with central block embellished with seated figure

rear wall, due to the discovery of a huge diagonal fault in the rock. This meant that the monument could never be used for worship.

To the left of the *chaitya* is Cave 25, a small rectangular cell containing a *stupa*, possibly the earliest excavation of the Amba Ambika Group. The *stupa* has a drum with tapering sides and post and railing ornament. The somewhat bulbous dome is topped with a *harmika*, from which rises a stone shaft, now broken, that once connected with the *chhatra* finial cut into the stone roof. To the right of the *chaitya* is Cave 27, a *vihara* comprising two cells sharing a common verandah. Cave 30 is part of a row of caves at a level of 1 to 2 metres higher that can be reached using a modern staircase. It appears that the two cells were later re-purposed and now house some roughly sculpted images, one of which represents the Jain goddess Ambika after whom this group of caves takes its name.

The Bhimshankar Group, the eastern most and last of the Manmodi monasteries to be described here, is of interest for its beautiful *Chaitya* (Cave 2). This comprises a virtually featureless, flat-roofed hall measuring some 10 by 3.5 metres. The doorway to the hall is set within a verandah with four octagonal pillars provided with pot and inverted-pyramidal capitals, all finished with care and clearly the work of skilled craftpersons. The pillars rise from a low balcony rendered in imitation of wooden counterparts with posts and railings, a design repeated on the upper balcony. The facade is crowned with a prominent *chaitya* window outline, unadorned except for shallow pilasters at either side; there is, however, no opening to admit light, the work evidently having been interrupted.

See also photograph on page 11

Visitors are recommended not to enter the *chaitya*, due to the presence of bees nests hanging over the entrance! The elongated, flat-roofed interior, lacking columns or aisles, leads to a rectangular monolithic mass extending from floor to ceiling, barely whittled to the form of a three-dimensional *stupa*. In recent times the mass has been cut and paint has been applied to sketch the form of a seated figure hailed as Bhimshankar, a form of Shiva, after whom this cluster of excavations now takes its name. This is the only flat-roofed hall intended to have a façade adorned with a *chaitya* window. Cave 1, the *vihara* immediately to the left, has a verandah with the same type of columns as those on the *chaitya*, except that the lack of balcony reveals the pot-shaped bases of the column shafts.

The other excavations of the Bhimshankar Group comprise *viharas*, with or without verandahs, many of them never full realized and of little architectural merit. That said, Cave 7, a tiny excavation, preserves an inscription recording a donation by Ayama, a minister of Nahapana. Why an important royal officer would have chosen to sponsor such a modest cave remains something of a mystery.

LENYADRI

Located 4 kilometres north of Junnar, Lenyadri is today a popular place of pilgrimage thanks to the shrine to Ganesha that now occupies one of the Buddhist *viharas*. As a result, visitors can access the ancient monastery halfway up the hill via a newly built staircase. The principal excavations are numbered from east to west.

Caves 1 and 2 are adjacent excavations, one with a small cell in the rear wall, the other with two cells, each entered through a small verandah, the one in Cave 1 provided with a small window.

Cave 5 is a much larger excavation, with an almost square hall measuring 7.5 by 8 metres, featuring seven cells cut into the side walls. The hall is fronted by a verandah, now mostly broken, with a doorway flanked by tiny windows. The inscription here records that the "satagabha" (seven-celled cave), along with its adjacent cistern, was a donation from the guild of corn-dealers.

The excavation of greatest architectural interest at the Lenyadri monastery is the *Chaitya* (Cave 6) with its well-finished interior. An inscription in characters of the early 2nd century CE on the rear wall of its verandah states that the "chetiyaghara" is the donation of a "single man" Sulasadata from Kalyana. The verandah is framed by four columns, with pot-shaped bases and tops, octagonal shafts and

inverted-pyramidal abacuses topped by pairs of animals, now much eroded. The *chaitya*-shaped recess on the cliff above the verandah has a smooth interior, suggesting that it was never intended to be cut out as a window. The semicircular-ended hall, more than 13 metres deep, has a central nave flanked by two rows of octagonal pillars. Five of these are similar to those in the verandah, with richly decorated bases and capitals adorned with pairs of fully modelled lions, tigers and elephants. The focal *stupa* is nearly 5 metres in height. A railing tops its drum and a *harmika* extends from the top of the stupa with an inverted-pyramidal abacus. The vault above the nave and the ceiling over the aisles on either side of the *stupa*, have well articulated, curving stone ribs imitating wooden construction.

Lenyadri, *Chaitya* (Cave 6)

ABOVE
Interior with *stupa*

OPPOSITE
Facade

The largest *vihara* among all those around Junnar is Cave 7 of Lenyadri. This *vihara* is entered through an imposing verandah of some size, with eight octagonal columns rising from a balcony embellished with relief posts and railings, that are now damaged. The columns have pot-shaped bases and tops, and inverted-pyramidal abacuses topped by pairs of lions, bulls, tigers and elephants with riders, though the details of the animals and humans can now hardly be made out. A doorway flanked by a window opening gives access to a rectangular hall, measuring more than 17 by 15 metres. This has nineteen cells, most with benches, cut into the side walls. The central cell in the rear wall is enlarged, and preceded by a low podium. Converted into a shrine to Ganesha, this central cell can no longer be accessed and the cave as a whole now forms an important Hindu shrine.

The next excavation of interest, Cave 14, is a rectangular, flat-roofed *chaitya*. Accessed through a verandah, the columns of which have worn away, the cave's *stupa* has a high cylindrical drum with railing. A *harmika* and an inverted-pyramidal abacus surmount the slightly bulbous dome, with a *chhatra* finial cut into the ceiling.

Cave 21 is a flat-roofed excavation entered through a verandah, the columns of which are now broken. The spacious hall has benches on three sides, but there are no cells. While the cave could, therefore, never have functioned as a monastic residence it may have served as a refectory or place of assembly. It will be impossible for visitors to continue beyond Cave 21, as there is no usable path.

Before returning to the bottom of the hill, visitors can pause by Caves 1 and 2 to obtain a distant prospect of the *Chaitya* (Cave 34) cut into the vertical cliff of a spur of Lenyadri hill to the east. With the aid of binoculars it is possible to make out the beautiful petalled design embellishing the frame of the great *chaitya* window that dominates the facade, as well as the crisply carved, relief *chaitya* arches on either side of the window's finial. Graffiti left by energetic rock climbers have been daubed onto the facade, and even onto the incomplete *stupa* within!

ABOVE
Lenyadri, *stupa* inside Cave 14

OPPOSITE
Lenyadri, *Chaitya* (Cave 34), facade

IN THE HEART OF THE GHATS

Bhaja, *Chaitya* (Cave 12), view

These four Buddhist sites in the heart of the Western Ghats are most easily reached from Lonavla, a popular resort town located in the Indrayani river valley, on National Highway 4, roughly midway between Mumbai and Pune. For visitors travelling from Pune, 65 kilometres from Lonavla, it is possible to visit Karla and Bhaja, the two most accessible monasteries, as single-day excursions. The name Lonavla, it should be pointed out, may derive from *lenauli*, which means "an abundance of *lenas* (caves)", no doubt referring to the monasteries described here.

Karla, *Chaitya* (Cave 8), facade, partly obscured by the modern Ekvira shrine

See also illustration on pages 6-7 and 33

KARLA

The monastery of Karla lies 11 kilometres east of Lonavla. A road running 3 kilometres north of the National Highway winds up to the car park, from which visitors must climb a steep but well-maintained path consisting of about 200 steps. Arriving at a broad terrace on the flank of the cliff, they will be greeted by a fine view of the Indrayani valley more than 100 metres below. Considerable crowds congregate here, not due to an interest in Karla's Buddhist heritage, but to pay their respects to Ekvira, a Hindu goddess who is the clan deity of the Koli fisherfolk of the Mumbai area, as well as being popular with the local population. A stone icon of Ekvira is housed in a simple cubical shrine with a pyramidal tiled roof dating back to the 18th century. Together with recent additions and ugly metal barriers to control pilgrims erected by the Koli Trust, the shrine partly obscures the front of the enormous *Chaitya* (Cave 8), the largest and most majestic early Buddhist monument in western Maharashtra.

One of the inscriptions at Karla states that "this mansion in stone, the best in Jambudvipe [India], paid for by the merchant Bhutapala". It appears unlikely that a single merchant could have financed such an ambitious project, and indeed the names of other donors found throughout the cave attest to a collaborative funding initiative. Among these are Ushavadata, son-in-law of Nahapana, the Kshatrapa ruler, and the Satavahana monarchs Gautamiputra Satakarni and Vasishthiputra Pulumavi. These 2nd-century CE royal inscriptions record donations of taxes and villages for the maintenance of the Buddhist community of Karla. However, by this date the *chaitya* had already been completed, either towards the end of the 1st century BCE or at the very beginning of the 1st century CE. Other inscriptions record

Karla, *Chaitya* (Cave 8), verandah with carvings of *mithuna* couples and elephants

gifts by lay donors as well as monks and nuns, possibly the result of direct solicitation by Karla's monastic community. Carbon 14 testing of the timber ribs set into the vaulted roof of the *chaitya* interior has yielded a chronological range from the 4th to the 1st centuries BCE.

As already outlined, Ekvira's shrine is the chief attraction for most visitors to Karla today. This is built over the stump of a monolithic column that formed one of a pair of identical columns cut out of the cliff to stand freely in front of the *chaitya*. That on the left, still preserved to its full height of almost 14 metres, has a tapering, sixteen-sided shaft surmounted by a fluted, bell-shaped capital supporting an inverted-pyramidal abacus and a quartet of lion torsos. The animals are shown with their feet apart, their fierce expressions accentuated by protruding tongues, glaring eyes and vigorous tufts of mane. It is possible that the lions originally served as the base for a *dharmachakra*, in imitation of Ashokan pillars that also feature stone wheels of this type, as may be seen in the sandstone fragments displayed in the Archaeological Museum in Sarnath outside Varanasi (Banaras). (It is worth noting that this Buddhist wheel is depicted on the Indian flag.) However, no remains of such an insignia have been discovered at Karla.

Behind these two free-standing columns lies a portion of a stone screen wall raised on two further octagonal pillars. Similar pillars surviving in the upper part of the cliff indicate that the screen would have continued across the whole width of the monument. Notches suggest the wall once held a timber frame that would have partly concealed the facade of the *chaitya* beyond. A verandah precedes the timber frame, and incorporates a great *chaitya* window with rock-cut ribs set into its sides, and portions of a ribbed wooden screen partly closing off the window's opening. The top of the window's arched frame is

KARLA

set within an architectural composition that features double tiers of balconies and smaller *chaitya* windows, all in shallow relief. Beneath the window lie three doorways giving access to the hall interior. Each doorway is topped with a *chaitya*-arched frame that reproduces on a smaller scale and in shallow relief the window above. The same is true of the relief representations of curving timber ribs within the frames. A frieze of railings, also in shallow relief, links the arched frames.

See also photographs on pages 3 and 39

Either side of the verandah doorways sit panels filled with *mithunas*, their fleshy torsos and limbs carved in deep relief. These male-female pairs are portrayed with smiling expressions in a variety of affectionate poses: with interlinked arms, one arm around the shoulder, gazing fondly towards each other, etc. Clad on their lower halves, in almost transparent garments, the males are shown with naked upper chests, the females with breasts exposed. Tassles and ornate belts with jewelled plaques secure their garments, and they wear bulky anklets, bracelets and earrings, and occasionally necklaces. Complicated turbans, with curious protuberances, evidently a fashion of the time, distinguish the males. These masterpieces of early Indian art contrast with more conventional Buddhist figures sculpted at a later date on the intermediate panels. The panel between the central and right-hand doorways shows a preaching Buddha on a lotus throne, its stalk clutched by diminutive *nagas*; the panel between the central and left-hand doorways depicts Avalokiteshvara holding a lotus. Attendants and flying celestial beings fill the sides and corners of both compositions. A row of smaller meditating and teaching Buddha figures can be seen above.

The 6-metre deep verandah has side walls that rise almost 20 metres to the ceiling. At the base of the walls on either side are three imposing elephant torsos carved with remarkable naturalism, with deeply modelled trunks and substantial, flapping ears. The panels with small Buddha figures over the elephant heads are a continuation of the later carvings on the main facade. The architectural compositions above have superimposed tiers of balconies and rows of horseshoe-shaped windows. The flat verandah ceiling is carved with ribs and rafters in imitation of timber construction, now much worn.

The magnificent dimensions and the almost perfect state of preservation of the *chaitya* interior cannot fail to impress visitors. The semicircular-ended hall extending almost 38 metres deep into the cliff and 14 metres wide, is divided into a nave and side aisles by two

lines of fourteen columns, most with pot bases, fluted, bell-shaped capitals and inverted-pyramidal abacuses. Each bracket comprises a pair of kneeling elephants with male and female riders. Within the side aisles, the elephants are replaced with horses. It is possible that the animals were enhanced with metal trappings, and that ivory tusks were affixed to the stone heads of the elephants (small holes can be seen). Unlike the *mithunas* on the *chaitya* facade, the human brackets are carved in the round, although only their upper bodies are visible. The close proximity of the animal-human capitals to each other creates an almost continuous sculpted frieze directing the eye to the great *stupa* that serves as a magnificent focus of the interior. Its imposing dome, almost 5 metres in diameter, is elevated on two superimposed drums, separated by a railing in shallow relief. The *harmika* with inverted-pyramidal abacus has a wooden post inserted into the top that carries the wooden *chhatra*, with a delicate lotus design carved onto the underside. The *chhatra* is an original feature, as are the timber ribs and intermediate rafters notched into the imposing vault that soars 14 metres above the floor. The ribs are aligned with each of the columns beneath, as well as being positioned in the intervening spaces; they are arranged in radial fashion above the *stupa*.

Karla, *Chaitya* (Cave 8), columns with animal-rider brackets inside the hall

See also photographs on page 5 and 26-27

It is worth noting several minor variations to the scheme just described. The four columns at the front of the hall, with plain octagonal shafts but no bases or capitals, support a gallery inside the *chaitya* window. The seven columns that define the aisle curving around the rear of the *stupa* are similarly plain. The eighth column on the right side of the nave has a sixteen-sided shaft engraved with shallow *stupa* flanked by a *dharmachakra* and a lion column in shallow relief, possibly reproducing the design of the great column outside.

After completing their tour of the *chaitya* visitors with remaining curiosity and time may wish to seek out several of the other fourteen excavations at Karla, most of which belong to a later period. Among the more interesting is Cave 4. This small flat-roofed *chaitya* is preceded by a verandah with four simple columns. A niche in the rear wall of its hall accommodates a relief carving of a preaching Buddha. Caves 11 to 15, cut at different levels into the cliff nearby have plain doorways leading to small cells. These simple caves are interesting not for their architectural merit but to help one imagine monastic life around the great *chaitya* all those years ago. Cave 14 contains two Buddha figures. Cave 15 has an inscription dated to the 24th year of the Satavahana monarch Vasishthiputra Pulumavi's reign (ca 154 CE). This mentions that the "navagabha matapa" (nine-celled hall) was donated for the benefit of the Mahasanghikas, a Buddhist sect that flourished in this part of the Deccan during the 2nd-3rd centuries.

BHAJA

A road running south for 5 kilometres from National Highway 4, directly opposite the one that leads to Karla, crosses a railway line and shortly after arrives at Bhaja, the next monastic site in the heart of the Western Ghats to be described here. From the car park a long stepped path climbs up to the entrance to the site. As the caves mostly face west, the afternoon is the best time to visit; during the monsoon, the view is enhanced by water spilling over the cliff face. For those with more time and energy there is a scenic but steep trek of about 2 hours from Bhaja to Lohagad fort above. This Maratha stronghold occupies the flat top of a rugged mountain more than 1,000 metres above sea level, from where there are magnificent views over the Indrayani valley below.

Dating back to the 2nd century BCE, the *chaitya* at Bhaja is regarded as one of the first and best preserved examples of its type in the Western Ghats. Indeed, many of the caves at Bhaja may be assigned to this period, comprising collectively one of the earliest Buddhist monasteries in the region. The caves are numbered from 1 to 26, in a north-to-south direction.

On arrival at the ticket office visitors will find themselves in front of the Chaitya (Cave 12), the most important of the Bhaja monuments. The imposing arched vault of the hall is almost 10 metres high, its curved opening lined with imitation timber ribs. Notches cut into the floor and side walls indicate that this was once closed off with a timber screen, no longer preserved. The arch is set within an architectural facade carved in relief on to the cliff face above and at either side. This depicts tiers of balconies with railings, partly supported on cut-out curved brackets, as well as *chaitya* windows, their interiors filled with curving timber screens, presumably imitating the actual screen that once filled the main arch. Tiny panels are filled with human couples with only their upper bodies visible, as if appearing in actual balconies.

More than 8 metres wide and 17 metres deep, the interior of the Bhaja *chaitya* is divided by columns into a nave and side aisles. The 27 columns are arranged in two rows that meet in a semi-circle behind the *stupa*. They have octagonal shafts that lean slight inwards, but are devoid of bases, capitals and brackets, all pointing to an early date for the monument. Timber ribs attached by notches in the vaulted roof

Bhaja, *Chaitya* (Cave 12), interior with *stupa*

See also photograph on pages 72-73

Bhaja,
Monolithic
stupas in Cave 20

*See also front
jacket*

over the central aisle continue in radial fashion above the *stupa*, giving
the impression of an actual wooden building. The *stupa* itself, 3 metres
in diameter, has a plain drum and dome. A small, cubical *harmika* with
railing motifs tops the dome with no finial.

The caves to the left of the *chaitya* are rudimentary excavations,
with cells cut into the internal walls of different shaped halls. They are in a
dilapidated condition and are not worth the attention of most visitors.
Of greater interest are the excavations immediately to the right, such as
Cave 13, which is a large rectangular *vihara*, its cell doorways headed with
finely carved *chaitya* arches set into railing reliefs. A staircase (restored)
leads the visitor up to two small *viharas*. Caves 15 and 16 feature traces
of *chaitya* arches that would have intersected with the main *chaitya's*
ornamentation.

Cave 20, a short distance away, comprises an artificially cut
overhang (restored) sheltering a cluster of fourteen monolithic *stupas*.
These are similar to that in the nearby *chaitya*, but considerably smaller
and incorporating railing designs. Worn inscriptions on several *stupas*
record the names of individuals, whose deaths these votive monuments
presumably honoured.

Cave 22 is a *vihara* of exceptional interest for its figural carvings.
From the outside the cave presents six slender columns (most are

reconstructions); a gap between the two on the left serves as an entrance. The interior of the verandah is roofed with a half-curved vault furnished with imitation wooden ribs and rafters, supported on a frieze of tiny *stupas* alongside figures with their arms held up. The vault gives the illusion of sheltering the rear wall of the verandah, which has two doorways and a single perforated window. Extending almost the full height of the walls flanking the doors are carvings of guardians dressed in elaborate military costume, one brandishing a long spear, the other a double-curved bow. A chamber cut into the left wall of the verandah has collapsed, leaving only an eroded frieze at the base showing male figures and horses, one of the animals provided with wings.

Bhaja, Cave 22, view

Particularly impressive are the relief panels on either side of the doorway to the cell cut into the verandah's right wall. The panel to the left shows a warrior holding the reigns of a chariot drawn by four horses, accompanied by a female wearing a rich headdress, and an attendant bearing a fly-whisk. The chariot is depicted as flying through the sky, suppressing a gigantic sprawling demon with convoluted limbs below. Other, smaller horse-riders can be made out on the upper right and on the left flanking wall. The panel to the right depicts another warrior accompanied by an attendant clutching three feathery staffs, both mounted on a huge, richly caparisoned elephant. The animal's trunk is uplifted to hold an uprooted tree; with one foot it presses down on another tree, much to the astonishment of tiny human figures beneath.

The interpretation of these unique panels in Cave 22's verandah remains one of the great puzzles of early Indian art. Some scholars have

Bhaja, Cave 22

ABOVE
Carvings of
military guardians
beside the
central verandah
doorway

RIGHT
Warriors
on a horse-
drawn chariot
(left) and an
elephant (right)
flanking the
side verandah
doorway

*See also
photograph on
page 41*

suggested that they represent Surya, the resplendent sun god, riding in his aerial chariot, on the left; and Indra, the god of the heavens atop the elephant, on the right. What purpose these Hindu gods could have had within the context of a Buddhist *vihara* has yet to be explained. Other specialists have argued that the reliefs illustrate popular Buddhist narratives known as *Jatakas*, though so far unidentified, or even an illustration of the story of Mandhata, a legendary king. In yet a further attempt at elucidation within a Buddhist context, other researchers have hypothesised that the rider in the chariot is suppressing the "enemies" of Buddhism, as personified in the wriggling body of the demon, while the rider on the elephant is a proud protagonist of Buddhism since his attendant holds a standard that bears a tiny *dharmachakra*. Such variant and frankly unconvincing interpretations, however, need not divert visitors from recognising the obvious regal spirit of these lively compositions, crowded as they are with warriors and attendants, a chariot and a war-elephant. Nor should they fail to notice the heavy ear ornaments, garlands, jewellery and elaborate headdresses, all typical attributes of the earliest phase of Indian figural art. A profusion of narrative sculptures of this type adorned the great *stupas* of Sanchi, Bharhut and Amaravati, however Bhaja offers one of the only examples in the rock-cut art of the Western Ghats. Exquisitely carved, these reliefs are among the greatest masterpieces from the 2nd century BCE.

The verandah of Cave 22 provides access to a modestly scaled, flat-roofed hall. (In order to gain access, however, visitors will have to ask for the key from the monument attendant.) The hall has two arched niches in the left wall, and two doorways leading to cells with rock-cut beds in the rear wall; a bench runs along the other side wall with guardians holding long spears (worn) either side of the central niche. The other two walls each have two doorways leading to cells with rock-cut beds. The niches and doorways are all

Bhaja, Cave 22,
interior cells

headed by deeply cut, well finished *chatiya* arches, complete with ribs on their curving inside faces, and relief screen designs within.

Of the remaining excavations at Bhaja, only Cave 26, the last in the series, needs to be described here. This is a small, roughly finished circular *chaitya* entered through an unadorned doorway. The central *stupa* has a plain drum and dome; a socket at the summit was provided for the separately carved *chhatra*, now lost.

BEDSA

Though perfectly accessible, this rock-cut monastery is not nearly as well known as Karla and Bhaja; nevertheless, the monastery is well worth visiting for its majestic and well preserved *chaitya* (Cave 7). The winding road that leads to Bedsa is located 12 kilometres east of the access roads to Karla and Bhaja. A long, steep flight of steps leads from the bottom of the hill to fifteen excavations cut into the east face of a cliff on the southern flank of the Pavna valley. Most of these are assigned to the 2nd-1st century BCE, with no evidence of occupation after the 1st century CE.

Caves 1 and 3 are both small circular *chaityas*, hardly more than 3 metres in diameter, now missing their front walls and ceilings. Beyond a pair of cisterns is the Chaitya (Cave 7), though almost completely concealed behind an uncut mass of rock. A narrow, roughly finished 12-metre long passageway leads directly to the *chaitya's* verandah which has four huge and magnificent columns, two standing freely, the other two engaged in the cliff at either side. The columns have pot bases, octagonal shafts and inverted-bell-shaped capitals with flutings. Each abacus has a tiny boxed-in *amalaka* and an inverted, stepped pyramid. Crowned with a pair of crouching elephants, horses or bulls, and ridden by a gesturing human couple, the abacuses are carved with remarkable precision. The figures appear to support the verandah ceiling carved with beams and rafters in imitation of a timber structure, rising more than 8 metres above the floor. The verandah's side walls have small cells with doorways topped by *chaitya* arches, repeated in relief in the tiers of cornices and balconies comprising the architectural facades above.

The imposing *chaitya* window in the verandah's rear wall is decorated with timber-like ribs set into its curving sides. Two doorways give access to the hall, with a single perforated stone window admitting additional light. These openings are each topped with *chaitya* arches containing relief representations of timber screens with curving timbers. Railing motifs run in between and at the base of the walls. The *chaitya's* semicircular-ended interior, 13.5 metres deep and about 6 metres wide, is divided into a nave and side aisles by two lines of columns consisting of octagonal shafts without bases and capitals. The curved vault rising 6.5 metres above the floor has faint notches for wooden ribs, though these have disappeared. The focal *stupa* is raised on two superimposed drums with relief railing friezes. The inverted-pyramidal abacus on top

Bedsa, *Chaitya* (Cave 7)

OPPOSITE
Facade partly obscured by an uncut mass of rock

FOLLOWING PAGES
Verandah doorways and windows

See also photographs on page 4, 30 and 37

Bhaja, Cave 11, interior

of the *harmika* above the dome has a separately carved stone post for a *chhatra* finial, presumably of wood, that is no longer present.

Passing by two cisterns, visitors should proceed to Cave 11, the principal dwelling of the Bedsa monastery, and possibly the first excavation at the site. Though now missing its verandah, the *vihara* plan is unique in featuring the semi-circular end usually found in a *chaitya*. The majority of the eleven cells cut into the curving walls are provided with a pair of rock-cut beds and the nine inner cells have doorways headed by relief *chaitya* arches linked by shallow railings. As in the nearby *chaitya*, the roof is fashioned as a curved vault with no supporting columns. The interior is almost 6 metres in both width and height, whilst being almost exactly twice this distance in depth. These measurements suggest that an ancient system of proportion regulated the design of the cave.

KONDANE

The monastery at this picturesque but remote forested site has two monuments, which, though ruined, are of outstanding architectural interest. Kondane is situated 13 kilometres from Karjat, a small town on the Ulhas river on the main Pune-Thane railway line, and about 5 kilometres east of Chauk, on National Highway 4. This location, on the western flank of the Western Ghats, is partly explained by the ancient trade route that followed the course of the Ulhas, linking Arabian Sea ports such as Sopara and Elephanta with the Deccan interior. In later times, the Marathas occupied this area, and an exciting though strenuous trek passes by Kondane on its way up to Rajmachi fort, scene of one of the key battles of the 18th-century Anglo-Maratha wars.

The caves that constitute the Kondane monastery are not associated with any known ancient settlement, suggesting that even in its heyday this was a secluded retreat. All the excavations belong to the 2nd century BCE, with little evidence of later work or occupation. One of the problems with preservation at the site is the deterioration of the geology: the lower portions of the caves were badly eroded, although many parts have now been restored by the local archaeological authorities.

The imposing *Chaitya* (Cave 1) makes any excursion to Kondane worthwhile. The cave is the rival of the Karla and Bedsa *chaityas* in scale and precision of carving, although unlike these other caves it lacks a verandah. The 8-metre wide opening of the hall has lost its side walls, but its *chaitya* arch remains preserved, complete with monolithic timber-like ribs lining its curving interior, as well as several curving struts of the wooden screen that once closed off the opening. The cliff face above and at the sides is fashioned into elaborate, multi-storeyed facades with superimposed tiers of railings and *chaitya* windows, some projecting outwards as balconies. Small panels either side of the main arch contain tiny warriors accompanied by dancing maidens. The role of these scenes in a Buddhist monument remains enigmatic. An inscription engraved onto the left wall of the *chaitya* facade records the name of Kanha, a disciple of Balaka, who "made the cave", perhaps a master architect or artist, or even a significant donor. The record is carved next to a high relief statue of a *yaksha*, his face now smashed, but with one unusual pointed ear and an ornate headscarf still plainly visible.

Now partly cleared of earth and collapsed rock, the interior of the Kondane *chaitya* has two rows of octagonal columns, without bases

FOLLOWING
PAGES
Kondane, *Chaitya*
(Cave 1) and
Cave 2, facade

*See also
photograph on
pages 8-9*

Kondane, Cave 2, interior

or capitals (restorations). These define the semicircular-ended interior some 22 metres deep, the curved vault rising 8.5 metres. The focal *stupa* within is badly eroded.

The adjacent *vihara* (Cave 2) comprises a spacious rectangular hall of 11 by 8.5 metres, its central space surrounded by columns, now mostly lost (some having been replaced by supporting struts). The gaps between the columns are aligned with small cells with doorways headed by relief *chaitya* arches. The most interesting aspect of the *vihara* is the ceiling that was originally supported by the columns that have just been described. Divided into panels by monolithic beams and rafters,

the ceiling evokes the interlocking components of an actual wooden structure. Of the verandah through which the hall was once entered, little can now be made out. However, its side walls partly survive, including that to the right, which has a *stupa* in full relief cut into an arched niche. Inscriptions carved onto the wall here record donations by Kamchikaputa and his son Dhamayakha.

    Of the other excavations at Kondane only Cave 8 needs to be described here. This small square *vihara* has a low bench running around two sides of the central space. One explanation for this plan is that the cave was excavated for a head monk or nun.

GREATER MUMBAI AND BEYOND

KANHERI

MAHAKALA

KUDA

Kanheri, Cave 67, relief carvings

Though the rock-cut monasteries at Kanheri and Mahakala are today embedded within the ever expanding metropolis of greater Mumbai, when the caves were first cut, and for the entire period that they were occupied by monks and nuns, they were situated on a series of islands lying a short distance off the Konkan coast. Easily accessible today from the metropolitan area, both monastic sites are worth visiting for their monumental architecture enhanced with figural reliefs and, in the case of Kanheri, its attractive forested locale.

The Kanheri and Mahakala monasteries were not the only Buddhist settlements in this part of the Deccan. *Stupas* at Sopara to the north (ancient Shurparaka) and Elephanta to the south indicate that several other monastic communities were active in the region. The presence of an Ashokan edict at Sopara attests to the area's commercial importance. As early as the 3rd-2nd century BCE these ports together with inland cities like Kalyan (ancient Kalyana) were linked by trade routes that wound their way through the rugged passes of the Western Ghats, via the monastic establishments of Karla, Bhaja, Bedsa, Nashik and Junnar, to the cities of Ter and Paithan in the Deccan plateau beyond.

See illustration on page 22

KANHERI

This monastic establishment, the most extensive in Maharashtra, is shielded from encroaching suburbs by the Sanjay Gandhi National Park, situated 40 kilometres north of central Mumbai. The National Park is conveniently reached by taxi or rickshaw from Borivali railway station on the main Churchgate line. From the entrance gate the road winds through pleasant forest for about 7 kilometres before reaching the car park from where visitors must proceed on foot. (Taxis and rickshaws are not admitted into the National Park, which provides its own, irregular bus service.)

The history of the Kanheri monastery begins in about the middle of the 2nd century CE, when it was called Kanhasela. This first phase of occupation, represented by some 75 caves, continued up until the beginning of the 4th century CE, during which period the site was patronised by the Satavahana kings and their representatives. In a second phase of activity, datable to the 5th-6th centuries, several older caves were modified and a number of new excavations were sponsored by the Traikutakas, then in control of the Konkan. Evidence for the

Kanheri, Caves overlooking the dry rivulet

involvement of these rulers is provided by a copper-plate inscription found in the vicinity of the *Chaitya* (Cave 3) dated to around 494 CE, as well as numerous Buddhist figures added to earlier excavations. These sculptural intrusions document the development of new forms of Buddhism possibly linked to the Mahayana doctrine that by this time was being adopted in the Deccan. A third and final phase from the 7th century onwards occurred under the Hindu Rashtrakutas and Shilaharas, who added little to the site.

Kanheri's chronology over this exceptionally long period testifies to the sustained support of Buddhist communities not only by local monarchs, but also by wealthy individuals involved in the lucrative Arabian Sea trade. Even after the invasion of the Deccan by the armies of the Delhi sultans at the end of the 12th century small bands of monks continued to reside in pockets of Kanheri's vast network of caves. However Buddhism did not survive the zeal of the Portuguese, who arrived on the coast in the 16th century. These new conquerors purportedly converted the remaining Buddhists at Kanheri to Christianity, and also inflicted considerable damage on the caves. In 1535 a Franciscan priest even attempted to convert the *chaitya* hall into a church dedicated to St. Michael!

Though there are more than 100 numbered caves at Kanheri only those of greatest architectural, artistic and historical interest are described here, as these may prove sufficient for most visitors with a single day at their disposal. The caves are described in numerical sequence, but visitors should consult the map inside the rear jacket of this volume to ascertain their somewhat random locations – next to a rivulet flowing with water only during the rainy months; and on the slopes of adjacent rugged basalt hills, especially that on the south. As they wander around the site, visitors should avail themselves of the many rock-cut benches in front of the caves and enjoy the refreshing panoramas of the forested National Park below. Rock-cut cisterns, some

See photograph on page 35

filled with water all year long, can be seen beside the paths, together with the channels that once conducted water to the monuments from catchments high up on the hills and from dams across the rivulet.

This account of the Kanheri monastery begins with the excavations strung along the western edge of the southern basalt hill that forms the core of the site. Cave 1, which appears to guard the entrance to the monastery, is one of the most imposing monuments

at Kanheri, but dates from no earlier than the 6th-7th century. Only its
verandah, with two squat proportioned columns with fluted shafts and
cushion capitals, and two plain engaged columns, was completed. The
screen wall beyond, with roughly cut doorways and windows at two
levels, was barely begun. The same is true of the facade of the *chaitya*
hall, with its roughly cut-out doorway and *chaitya* window above. As for
the cave's interior, this was abandoned at an early stage, though the
process of cutting revealed a tunnel-like cutting deep into the hillside.

Cave 2 comprises two adjoining chambers and a large *vihara*,
now all missing their front walls, leaving only an artificially cut, projecting
ledge above. The first chamber has a monolithic *stupa* embellished
with a rudimentary post-and-railing frieze and a *harmika*, with a seated
Buddha carved onto the rear wall. The *stupa* in the second chamber is
altogether plain, but preserves traces of polish on its dome, suggesting a

Kanheri, Cave 1,
facade

3rd-2nd-century BCE date, making it one of the earliest caves at Kanheri. Later carvings on rear walls depict preaching Buddhas, as well as large Bodhisattvas holding lotuses with trailing stalks. The Avalokiteshvara panel on the rear wall includes the perils from which devotees are to be rescued. The adjacent *vihara* is more than 16 metres wide, and has two doorways for cells cut into the rear wall. A two-line inscription of the 2nd century CE on the wall between the doorways record "meritorious gifts" by Nakanaka of Nashik and the goldsmith Samidita of Kalyana.

By far the largest and most impressive excavation at Kanheri is the great *Chaitya* (Cave 3). According to an inscription carved on the right-hand gatepost of the *chatiya's* screen wall, two merchant brothers, Gajasena and Gajamitra, completed the monument during the reign of Yajnashri Satakarni, a later Satavahana monarch (r. ca 172-201). The record is of interest since it refers to an overseer, a stone mason and a stone-polisher, all of whom must have played vital roles in cutting the cave. The cave remains unfinished and appears to have been cut over several phases, the earliest some years before the reign of Yajnashri but after the completion of the *chaitya* at Karla, which it imitates.

See photograph on
page 18

The Kanheri *chaitya* is preceded by a court defined by a low wall carved with an ornamental railing of posts and railings decorated with floral roundels, with a row of animals set beneath that are now worn. Bulky male guardians, one hand placed firmly on the hip (the heads now missing), flank the entrance in the middle of the railing. More complete

is the *naga* figure holding up a flower, at the extreme right of the wall. Lofty columns with octagonal shafts, around 9 metres in height, are partly cut out of the cliff on either side of the court within. The square column bases are carved with tiny male figures, some standing with one hand raised up, others seated with *naga* hoods. The figures at the base of the shaft of the right-hand column depicting Buddha flanked by Bodhisattvas are among the earliest such representations in Deccan art. Circular, cushion-like capitals and inverted, stepped-pyramidal abacuses surmount the column shafts. The capitals are fashioned as seated lions (right) or pot-bellied dwarfs (left). A chamber cut at a later date into the left wall of the court is approached through a vestibule adorned with standing Buddha figures that are larger than life size.

The facade of the *chaitya* hall is partly concealed from the court by a stone screen with four supports and five rectangular openings above (what can be seen today is partly restored). Deep notches suggest that the screen was once embellished with timbers. Inscriptions cover the inner faces of the screen's central two gateposts, between which visitors pass in order to enter the hall's verandah. Large panels carved with pairs of *mithunas* occupy the wall surfaces either side of the three

Kanheri, *Chaitya* (Cave 3)

RIGHT
Wall panel with *mithuna* couples in the verandah

OPPOSITE
Buddha figure in the side niche of the verandah

FOLLOWING PAGES
Interior with *stupa*

BUDDHIST ROCK-CUT MONASTERIES

doorways at the rear. (These bear a close resemblance to similar *mithunas* at Karla.) Depicted in full relief, the men with broad chests, the women with heavy breasts, they are dressed in garments with pleated sashes and adorned with bulky necklaces and ear ornaments, and sport elaborate hairdos and headdresses; the males hold a lotus flower in one hand. The horseshoe-shaped opening above the doorways is blocked out, and was never fashioned into a standard *chaitya* window. The verandah's side walls are each filled with a colossal Buddha figure, 6.5 metres high, added in the 5th-6th century. The Master stands within a deep niche headed by an arch with floral bands issuing from open-mouthed *makaras* or sea creatures. The space above is filled with celestial couples, their legs kicked back in the act of flying through the heavens. Tiny figures at the apexes of the arches worship a vase with a flowering lotus (left) or a funerary urn (right). The Buddhas have their right hands opening outwards and down, in the gesture of bestowing boons, known as *varada-mudra*; their left hands clutch the upper fold of their diaphanous garments, the edges of which flow across their lower legs. The deep carving and smooth modelling of the body, the serene facial expression, and the subtle swaying posture with one leg advanced slightly, are typical features of Buddhist art as perfected in the Deccan under Vakataka sponsorship, and exemplified by the art of the Ajanta monastery in the late 5th century. (It not impossible that Ajanta artists were employed here.) Numerous smaller Buddhist images are added along the verandah walls, their irregular placing betraying a lack of coordinated planning.

The apsidal end of the interior of Kanheri's *chaitya* is of ample size, measuring 26 metres deep and 13.5 metres wide. It is divided into nave and side aisles by two lines of massive octagonal columns, 34 in all. Only the first six columns on both sides of the nave have pot bases, though these and the next four columns on the left all have cushion-like capitals topped with riders on animals. The rest of the columns lack these features, though several are of interest for the scenes of *stupa* worship and footprints beneath the *bodhi* tree engraved on to their shafts, probably at some later date. The vaulted roof that soars some 13 metres above the floor was provided with timber ribs, today evidenced only by deep notches. The unadorned, hemispherical *stupa*, almost 5 metres in diameter and more than 6.5 metres high, elevated on a tall, unadorned cylindrical drum, provides a dramatic focus for the majestic but austere interior.

Two structural brick *stupas* were discovered in front of the *chaitya* hall, but only the square plinth of moulded bricks of one now remains. Copper urns containing relics and the dated copper-plate inscription mentioned earlier were recovered from these *stupas*

Immediately to the left of the great *chaitya* is Cave 4. This tiny, circular *chaitya*, less than 4 metres in diameter, belongs to the earliest phase at Kanheri. At a later date, however, its *stupa* with a bulbous dome, had intrusive seated Buddhas carved onto its cylindrical base. Similar images are seen on the curving walls to the rear. The *harmika* connected to the *chhatra* is cut into the flat ceiling above.

From these first caves at Kanheri visitors should follow the stepped path running beside the central rivulet that descends through the site. The next excavation of any size to be noticed is Cave 10. Its five-bayed verandah incorporates three doorways in the rear wall, but the hall within is greatly dilapidated. A flight of steps to one side climbs to the Darbar Hall (Cave 11), which faces north on to a spacious court provided with two small cisterns. Its extremely long verandah features eight octagonal columns and two square engaged columns, approached by three flights of steps. The left end of the verandah has a small chamber fronted by slender columns with partly fluted shafts

Kanheri, Darbar Hall (Cave 11)

See also photograph of interior on page 24

and cushion capitals. Its rear and side walls are carved with preaching Buddhas flanked by standing Bodhisattvas.

Three doorways inside the verandah of Cave 11 access the hall's spacious interior, measuring more than 22 metres in width and almost 10 metres in depth. Two low, parallel plinths in the middle of the floor run almost the full width of the hall. These probably served as benches for monks to sit at while studying and reciting sacred texts. (Similar benches are seen in the Buddhist Cave 5 at Ellora.) A sanctuary in the middle of the rear wall accommodates a preaching Buddha between Bodhisattvas, with flying celestial carvings above. Colonnades at either side have doorways with small cells; cell doorways are also seen in the colonnade on the left, but not in that on the right.

An inscription on the cliff face above the left-hand cistern of Cave 11's court mentions Kapardin, a Shilahara prince associated with the Rashtrakuta king Amoghavarsha. Listing various gifts as well as funds for the purchase of books, the record confirms that the purpose of the cave was a place of study. Though it bears a date equivalent to 853 CE, the similarities with Cave 5 at Ellora suggest that it was already in use during the 5th-6th century.

Cave 12 on the opposite side of the path that runs past Cave 11 is entered through a verandah with columns that consist of part-circular fluted shafts and cushion capitals, typical of 6th-century Deccan architecture. The verandah gives access to a small square hall with a cell at the rear accommodating a seated Buddha.

The path beside the rivulet continues past several more excavations. They include Cave 32, which has a hall door and windows, preceded by a verandah with columns raised on a low parapet wall enlivened with railing motifs. The square hall within has benches running around two sides. An inscription in the verandah records that a donor from Kalyana gifted the *lena*, together with its seating benches and adjacent cisterns, as well as income to provide clothes and shoes for the inhabitants.

Nearby Cave 34 has a verandah with two full columns and two engaged columns with unusual etched circles on the shafts, separated by sixteen-sided, fluted sections, and stepped brackets. A single doorway offers access to a rectangular hall with single cells in the side walls. A triple-bayed portico at the rear then leads on to a narrow vestibule, of interest for the fully modelled standing Buddhas carved onto the walls. The

Kanheri, Cave 41, Seated Buddha in side chamber

painting on the ceiling here is the only example of mural art at Kanheri, or indeed at any early Buddhist site in the Western Ghats. This depicts the outline of a seated Buddha, marked with guidelines indicating the correct proportions to be followed, but only partly coloured in. The cell in the sanctuary beyond has a pedestal, but filled with no image.

For mural art in Kanheri, see photograph of Cave 34 on page 43

Cave 36, a short distance further along the path, is a small circular, flat-roofed *chaitya* housing a monolithic *stupa*. Its bulbous dome carries a *harmika* that touches the *chhatra* carved onto the ceiling. Traces of plaster indicate that the ceiling was once painted.

Cave 41, the next *vihara* at Kanheri on this path to be described here, is of interest for the small chamber cut into the right side of the court. Within the chamber, a seated Buddha accompanied by Bodhisattvas is sculpted onto the rear wall. The left-hand saviour is provided with eleven heads, an iconographic peculiarity found nowhere else in India, though apparently known in China in the 7th-8th centuries. The appearance of this unique icon at Kanheri remains something of a mystery. The cave itself is entered through a projecting portico with four slender columns carrying cushion capitals, raised on a low moulded basement approached by steps. A single doorway gives access to a square hall with cell doorways on two sides. The shrine set into the rear wall accommodates the usual trio of seated Buddha and standing Bodhisattvas.

After Cave 41 the path makes a turn to cross over a broken stone wall that served as a dam to trap the rivulet's water. The path on this

side of the rivulet passes by another line of excavations that includes Cave 21. This simple *vihara* has a verandah, now missing its columns. The doorway, flanked by windows with tiny perforations, provides access to a square hall with benches running around two sides. An inscription records that a donor from Kalyana donated the monument during the 16th year of Yajnashri Satakarni's reign (ca 188 CE).

The other caves at Kanheri described here are located at different heights along the stepped paths that run around and over the steeply sloping flank of the great hill south of the rivulet. Most of these are *viharas* that face wedge-shaped openings scooped out of the basalt mass. These openings are fashioned into courts provided with cisterns and benches. The caves have columned verandahs, sometimes with low parapet walls, that lead into square halls, often with low seating on two or three sides.

Cave 67 is one of the largest and most artistically interesting of these *viharas*. The cave faces into a court flanked by long benches, with a cistern cut into the left wall of the cliff and a small chamber opposite. A flight of steps flanked by balustrades ascends to the five-bayed verandah, supported by octagonal columns raised on low walls embellished with posts and railings in relief. The rear wall of the verandah is festooned

Kanheri, Cave 67

OPPOSITE
Court in front of
the verandah

BELOW
Interior

*See also
photographs on
pages 98-99*

with Buddhas seated on lotus flowers with stalks gripped by crouching *nagas*, that are in turn surrounded by smaller Buddha figures. The right end wall of the verandah portrays Avalokiteshvara flanked by two female attendants. Three doorways in the rear wall give access to a hall, more than 14 metres wide and 12 metres deep, with low benches running around three sides. Two doorways lead to cells in each of the side walls. The rear and side walls are altogether covered with Buddha images seated in recesses of different sizes, some headed by semicircles. These alternate with larger standing Buddhas, their hands in the gesture of *varada-mudra*, as well as larger Buddhas seated on lotuses clutched by *nagas* (snake deities).

Kanheri, Cave 90, throne for Buddha figure, now missing

See also photograph on page 42

Cave 69 is of interest for its aberrant layout, perhaps intended both as a residence for an important teacher and a classroom for his students. This has a five-bayed verandah with steps not in the middle, but to one side that lead to a doorway in its rear wall offering access to

a square hall with seating on two sides and illuminated by two windows. A doorway on the left leads to a small chamber, also with seating on two sides and lit by a window.

The comparatively small Cave 90 is worth seeking out for its sculpted compositions, among the best preserved at Kanheri. The triple-bayed verandah with simple octagonal columns is accessed by a flight of worn steps. Its rear and end walls are covered with Buddha figures, both larger standing and smaller seated. One composition at the base of the walls shows the Master seated between a female devotee and a tiny *stupa*. A single doorway leads into the square hall, into the back of which has been cut a full-height recess flanked by tall Bodhisattvas topped by flying couples. The recess contains a large halo in relief and a deep groove to secure a separately carved stone image, now lost.

The right side wall of the hall shows standing Avalokiteshvara holding a prominent lotus blossom flanked by female attendants, sometimes identified as Tara and Bhrikti. At either side are small scenes depicting the salvation of devotees from the Eight Perils, including attacks by elephants, lions and robbers, and even deliverance from shipwreck, together with two large standing Buddhas. On the left side wall there is a panel of Buddha seated on a prominent lotus, the stalk held by gods above, sometimes identified as Indra and Brahma, in rapt attention, with *nagas* beneath. Attendants holding fly-whisks flank the figures, including females and others. To some interpreters this crowded composition expresses the Master's universal knowledge emanating from the four quarters, in accordance with Mahayana beliefs.

The last Kanheri excavation to be described here is Cave 101, which repeats the scheme already discussed for Cave 69. The benches on the side walls of the court in front have unusual, elegantly curved end-rests. Cisterns are seen at either side.

Visitors to Kanheri with remaining curiosity and energy should seek out the Buddhist Cemetery on the other side of the hill, about 750 metres south of the caves just described. The path to the cemetery, which can also be reached directly from the car park, is narrow and perilous as it skirts a deep ravine; a guide is recommended. The path terminates in a natural overhang that shelters several lines of small structural brick *stupas*, now severely dilapidated.

FOLLOWING PAGES
Brick *stupas* in the Buddhist cemetery at Kanheri

MAHAKALA

Known also as Kondivte, this monastery 10 kilometres southwest of Kanheri is most conveniently reached from the Jogeshwari-Vikhroli Link Road, or from Andheri railway station, 6 kilometres to the west. Some twenty caves at this site are cut into the sides of a single basalt outcrop, the most important situated in a row along its eastern face. Of these, the *Chaitya (Cave 9)* is of greatest interest: its unique plan suggests that it dates to around the end of the 2nd century BCE, making it one of the earliest rock-cut monuments in Maharashtra. This *chaitya* comprises a long hall, now missing its front wall, leading to a circular shrine with overhanging eaves, mimicking with remarkable faithfulness a free-standing, circular thatched hut. Windows with simple, square perforations flank its doorway. An inscription of the 2nd century CE, presumably a later dedication, is cut beside the right-hand window.

Mahakala, *Chaitya* (Cave 9), interior with circular stupa chamber

The shrine within, some 4.5 metres in diameter, is roofed with a dome scooped out of the rock, but now missing its radial, timber ribs. This accommodates a monolithic *stupa* that takes up most of the internal space. On the right wall of the hall in front are several figures added in the 5th-6th centuries. They include the preaching Buddha attended by Bodhisattvas.

Mahakala caves 13 and 14

   Other monuments at Mahakala were only excavated in the 5th-6th centuries. Cave 2 has a columned verandah leading to a rectangular hall that may have served as a *chaitya* since there is a pedestal with a relief *stupa* cut into the rear wall. Cave 4 is a *vihara* with a columned verandah featuring benches, and a square hall with columned corridors cut into the side and rear walls, each corridor giving access to a set of three cells. Cave 13 is more unusual since it has a columned verandah, a hall with four columns in the middle arranged in a square, and eight cells, some with beds, on three sides, as well as a shrine in the rear wall, with an empty pedestal. The right wall of the court in front has a recess with a cistern.

KUDA

The monastery at Kuda consists of 24 caves making it the most extensive of several Buddhist rock-cut monasteries dotted along the Konkan coastal strip south of Mumbai. However, it is the only one of these monasteries to be described here, in the hope that it will attract visitors from nearby Murud, a popular seaside destination, often visited due to the nearby island fort of Janjira. Kuda lies 12 kilometres south-east of Murud, on the southern bank of the Murud-Janjira estuary, near the village of Mandad, the latter described by many scholars as the ancient port of Mandagora, an important node in the ancient Indian Ocean trade network. The monastery commands a beautiful perspective over the Arabian Sea and the well tended caves are situated close to the road, 50 metres along a clearly marked path.

Cave 6, the largest of the 24 excavations at Kuda, is a flat-roofed *chaitya* entered through a court, one side of which is carved with a majestic elephant torso in full relief and close to full size! Beautiful

mithunas are carved onto the walls at the far end of the flat-roofed hall that precedes a shrine accommodating a monolithic *stupa*. The Kuda figures are shown in the same postures and display similar garments, jewellery and headdresses as those on the verandah walls at Karla. However, they are probably not contemporary with the Karla figures, but copies of the 2nd-3rd centuries. Intrusive carvings of the 5th-6th century on the side walls of the hall show multiple teaching Buddhas, including several of the Master seated on a lotus with a long stalk held by *nagas*. Smaller versions of these compositions are also cut on the walls either side of the cave's verandah, which has octagonal columns rising on a low balustrade wall decorated with clearly preserved railing motifs. The access steps in the middle, however, are altogether worn.

Caves 1, 9 15 and 21 are also flat-roofed *chaityas* with *stupas*, approached through verandahs and halls, but devoid of carvings from any period. Cave 4 has the largest hall of any excavation, measuring almost 17 by 10 metres, but featuring no *stupa*.

Kuda, Cave 6

ABOVE
Carvings inside
the hall

OPPOSITE
Verandah

CHRONOLOGY OF THE CAVES

The periodization given here summarises recent scholarship. It provides dates according to the long Satavahana chronology.

PERIOD ONE: 250 BCE TO 120 CE
This period is marked by the rule of the Satavahanas in western Maharashtra, as attested by inscriptions that mention Krishna (r. ca 205-187 BCE) and Satakarni (r. ca. 187-177 BCE). The latter half of the period witnesses the growing power of the Kshatrapas in neighbouring Gujarat, and the period ends just prior to the conflict between the two dynasties over control of this part of India.

> Nashik, Pandu Lena, 18 (*chatiya*), 19
> Junnar, Bhutling 40 (*chaitya*), 45;
> Lenyadri 34 (*chaitya*); Tulja Lena 2
> (*chaitya*), 3, 15, 16
> Karla 8 (*chaitya*)
> Bhaja 12 (*chaitya*), 3, 15, 16, 22, 26 (*chaitya*)
> Bedsa 7 (*chaitya*), 11
> Kondane 1 (*chaitya*), 2
> Kanheri 3 (*chaitya*)
> Mahakala 9 (*chaitya*)

PERIOD TWO: 120 TO 200
The early years of this period are dominated by the conflict between the Satavahanas and Kshatrapas, the impact of which is recorded in inscriptions mentioning the Satavahana king Gautamiputra Satakarni (r. ca 106-130) and the Kshatrapa ruler Nahapana (r. ca 106-124). By 124 Satakarni defeats Nahapana and restores Satavahana rule over western Maharashtra. The period ends with the reign of Yajnashri Satakarni (r. ca 172-201).

> Nashik, Pandu Lena 3, 10, 20, 23
> Junnar, Bhimshankar 2 (*chaitya*), 7;
> Amba Ambika 26 (*chaitya*); Lenyadri 6
> (*chaitya*), 7 (courtyard *vihara*)
> Karla 15
> Kanheri 21
> Kuda 9 to 14, followed by 15 to 19.

PERIOD THREE: 200 TO 400
These years witness the gradual fragmentation of Satavahana rule in western Maharashtra. Several local rulers rise to prominence, such as the Mahabhojas.

> Junnar, Shivneri, 42, 43 (*chaitya*); Amba
> Ambika, 25 (*chaitya*)
> Kanheri, 36, 101
> Kuda, 20 to 26, followed by 1 to 7

PERIOD FOUR: 400 TO 1,000
At the beginning of this period the Vakatakas rise to prominence in central India, and their patronage of the monasteries at Ajanta in northern Maharashtra influenced Nashik, Karla and Kanheri. Later rulers of consequence in the region are the Rashtrakutas and local dynasties in western Maharashtra, like the Shilaharas.

> Nashik, Pandu Lena, additions to 2, 17,
> 20, 23, 24
> Karla, 4, 14
> Kanheri, 1, 4, 11, 34, 41, 67, 90 , 101

BIBLIOGRAPHY

Alone, Y.S., *Buddhist Caves of Western India: Forms and Patronage*, New Delhi: Kaveri Books, 2016.

Brancaccio, Pia, ed., *Living Rock: Buddhist, Hindu and Jain Cave Temples in the Western Deccan*, Mumbai: Marg Foundation, 2013.

Dehejia, Vidya, *Early Buddhist Rock Temples: A Chronological Study*, London: Thames and Hudson, 1972.

Dehejia, Vidya and Peter Rockwell, *The Unfinished: Stone Carvers at Work on the Indian Subcontinent*, New Delhi: Roli Books, 2016.

Dhavalikar, M.K., *Late Hinayana Caves of Western India*, Poona: Deccan College of Postgraduate and Research Institute, 1984.

Fisher, Robert E., *Buddhist Art and Architecture*, London: Thames and Hudson, 1993, Chapter One.

Fergusson, James and James Burgess, *The Cave Temples of India*, reprint, Delhi: Oriental Books, 1969.

Harle, J.C., *The Art and Architecture of the Indian Subcontinent*, Harmondsworth: Penguin, 1986, Chapter 2.

Huntington, Susan L., *The Art of Ancient India: Buddhist, Hindu, Jain*, New York and Tokyo: Weatherhill, 1985, Chapters 5, 9 and 12.

Kail, Owen, *Buddhist Cave Temples of India*, Bombay: Taraporevala, 1975.

Margabhandu, C., *Archaeology of the Satavahana Kshatrapa Times*, Delhi: Sundeep Prakashan, 1985.

Mirashi, Vasudev Vishnu, *The History and Inscriptions of the Satavahanas and the Western Kshatrapas*, Bombay: Maharashtra State Board for Literature and Culture, 1981.

Mitra, Debala, *Buddhist Monuments*, Calcutta: Sahitya Samsad, 1980.

Nagaraju, S., *Buddhist Architecture of Western India (c. 250 B.C. – c. A.D. 300)*, Delhi: Agam Kala Prakashan, 1981.

Ray, Himanshu P., *Monastery and Guild: Commerce Under the Satavahanas,* New Delhi, Oxford University Press, 1986.

Rees, Gethin, "Colonial Discourse: Indian Ocean Trade and the Urbanisation of the Western Deccan", *South Asian Studies*, 30/1 (2014).

-----, "Rivers, Valleys, Plains and the Distribution of the Rock-cut Monasteries of the Western Ghats", in D.K. Chakrabarti and M. Lal, eds., *History of Ancient India,* New Delhi: Aryan Books, 2014.

Sarkar, H., *Studies in Early Buddhist Architecture of India*, Delhi: Munshiram Manoharlal, 1966.

Shastri, Ajay Mitra., *The Satavahanas and the Western Kshatrapas: A Historical Framework*, Nagpur: Dattsons, 1998.

----, *The Age of the Satavahanas*, New Delhi: Aryan Books, 1999.

Yazdani, Gulam, ed., *The Early History of the Deccan*, London: Oxford University Press, 2 volumes, 1960.

GLOSSARY

amalaka, ribbed fruit-like motif used as a capping motif in a column abacus

Ashoka, 3rd century BCE Maurya emperor of northern India

Avalokiteshvara, popular Bodhisattva

bodhi, the tree beneath which Buddha sat to attain enlightenment

Bodhisattva, compassionate saviour figure of later Buddhism

Brahmi, script of the inscriptions in the early rock-cut monasteries

Buddha, founder of Buddhism in the 6th-5th centuries BCE; later worshipped as a divinity

chaitya, a shrine accommodating a votive *stupa*; a window or ornamental arch with a distinctive horseshoe-shaped profile associated with a *chaitya* shrine

chetiya, Pali for *chaitya*

chhatra, umbrella finial of a *stupa*

Deccan, elevated plateau region of peninsular India

dhamma, Pali for *dharma*

dharma, the Buddhist doctrine

dharmachakra, spoked wheel symbolising Buddha's first sermon at Sarnath

dharmachakra-mudra, hand gesture of Buddha preaching

Ekvira, Hindu goddess worshipped at Karla

Gautamiputra Satarkarni, Satavahana king

ghat, step; name of the mountain ranges bordering India's Deccan plateau

harmika, ornamental railing that supports a *stupa*

Indra, god of the heavens *Jatakas*, Indian popular folk tales incorporated into Buddhist lore

Konkan, coastal strip between the Arabian Sea and the Western Ghats

Krishna, Satavahana king

Kshatrapas, dynasty that controlled Gujarat and northern Maharashtra between the 1st century BCE and 1st century CE

Lakshmi, goddess of wealth and good fortune

lena, cave

Mahayana, later phase of Buddhism that focused on the veneration of images of Buddha and Bodhisattvas

Mahasanghika, early sect of Buddhism in the Deccan

mandala, auspicious geometric diagram as an aid for meditation

Nahapana, Kshatrapa king

mithuna, auspicious human couple

naga, semi-divine serpent being, usually shown with a human body sheltered by cobra hoods

Padmapani, Lord of the Lotus, popular Bodhisattva

Pali, preferred language of early Buddhism

pradakshina, circumambulatory rite

Rashtrakutas, dynasty ruling the Deccan during the 8th-10th centuries

sangha, Buddhist monastic community

Satavahanas, dynasty ruling the Deccan between the 2nd century BCE and 2nd century CE

Shilaharas, rulers of the southwestern
Deccan during the 9th-11th centuries
stupa, hemispherical funerary mound that
came to be worshipped as a symbol of
Buddha and his teachings
Surya, sun god
torana, portal with two posts supporting
one or more horizontal lintels
Traikutakas, rulers of the Konkan during
the 5th-6th centuries
uposatha, monastic ceremony
varada-mudra, hand gesture of granting
blessings

Vasishthiputra Pulumavi, Satavahana king
vihara, residence for Buddhist monks or
nuns, generally providing sleeping cells
with beds
Western Ghats, range of mountains
between the Arabian Sea and the Deccan
plateau
Yajnashri Satakarni, Satavahana king
yaksha, yakshi, semi-divine male and female
spirit
yavana, merchant of Greek-origin; term
later used to designate any foreigner

INDEX

Mostly restricted to names, sites and monuments.
Page numbers in colour have illustrations